A frontispiece designed in 1792 by the architect Manuel Ruiz. (Courtesy of the Archivo General de la Nación.)

Architectural Practice
in Mexico City

*A Manual for Journeyman Architects
of the Eighteenth Century*

*Translated, with an Introduction and Annotation,
by* MARDITH K. SCHUETZ

THE UNIVERSITY OF ARIZONA PRESS
TUCSON

THE UNIVERSITY OF ARIZONA PRESS
Copyright © 1987
The Arizona Board of Regents
All Rights Reserved

This book was set in 10/13 Linotron 202 Galliard.
Manufactured in the U.S.A.

Library of Congress Cataloging-in-Publication Data

Architectural practice in Mexico City.

Translation of: Architectura mechanica conforme la practica
de esta Ciudad de Mexico.
English and Spanish.
Bibliography: p.
Includes index.
1. Architectural practice—Mexico—Mexico City—
Handbooks, manuals, etc.—Early works to 1800.
2. Architectural practice—Mexico—Mexico City—
History—18th century—Sources. I. Schuetz,
Mardith K. II. Architectura mechanica conforme
la practica de esta Ciudad de Mexico. 1987.
NA1996.A7315 1987   720   87-3456
ISBN 0-8165-1000-8 (alk. paper)

British Library Cataloguing in Publication data are available.

This book is dedicated to my parents
Thomas Graves Keithly and Amy Miller Keithly

Contents

Foreword

Important discoveries often occur by chance. While doing some research on a Mexican painting of the Virgin of Valvanera, I happened to ask a friend who had a small collection of Mexican colonial engravings and imprints if he might have anything related to my topic. As it happened, he did have one book, and when he brought me that volume he also brought along with it the manuscript which is being published here. He had found the manuscript on the shelf near the book for which he was searching; it was something even he had forgotten he had. My friend acquired this manuscript, *Architectura mechanica conforme la practica de esta Ciudad de México*, in 1963 from Dawson's Book Shop in Los Angeles. The shop was disposing of some material from the estate of the Mexican priest and bibliographer Emilio Valtón, who appears to have been the source of the document, although neither Father Valtón nor my friend was aware of the uniqueness of the manuscript. Nothing is known of its history from the time of its probable ownership by Manuel Barona up until its acquisition by Valtón; it is not even known when or under what circumstances Valtón acquired it. The present owner of the manuscript prefers to retain his anonymity.

The manuscript now consists of forty-four sewn pages of eighteenth-century paper bound in thin pasteboard covers of the sort typically used on books sold at a cheaper price than those bound in leather or parchment. The covers are decorated with a sort of rudimentary marbleizing in brownish purple. The first three sheets are blank on their reverse sides. Other blank pages presumably were subsequently removed, as were an uncertain number of pages with architectural drawings. No architectural drawings now accompany the text. However, there are a number of decorations in red, or in red, green, and brown, which make the manuscript a minor work of art. The writing, done in brown ink, appears to be by a single hand, and a reasonably skilled one at that. All but two pages also have writing or ornamentation in red ink. The title page has some green ink as well. Most of the ornamentation bears little resemblance to book ornamentation, though there is some reminiscent of the illumination of great choral books. Rather, the ornamentation of the title page more closely resembles baroque wall decorations. Many of the capital letters are flamboyantly calligraphic, and on two pages section heads are adorned with birds and flowers of a rather spectacular nature. In fact, the scribe seems to have been carried away by his enthusiasm. There is a sketch on the sheet following the title page that bears the signature of a later owner, Manuel Barona, which is by a different, unskilled hand. The book does not seem to be a copy of another work; the author either decided not to include his name or he put it on a sheet that is now lost.

Although I was encouraged to do the translation of this work myself, I felt that it would be more desirable if it were done by someone more acquainted with the trade of the builder in Mexico, and Mardith Schuetz seemed to be the most qualified. The choice was eminently a correct one.

NORMAN NEUERBURG

Acknowledgments

A book of this sort can materialize only through the nurturing of many individuals who share a common belief that such a work should be made available to architectural historians and general scholars of New World history. I therefore acknowledge those who have collaborated in one way or another to help me produce this edition of *Architectural Practice in Mexico City*.

My thanks first go to the owner of the manuscript and to Norman Neuerburg, who entrusted me with the job of translating and annotating this unique work. Elizabeth Wilder Weismann and Barbara Anderson read my manuscript and offered valuable comments and suggestions. María del Carmen Olvera C. allowed her fine set of eighteenth-century drafting instruments to be photographed, and she volunteered her time to compare the handwriting of the manual's author with that of known eighteenth-century architects in an unfortunately unsuccessful attempt to identify the author. Richard Jensen of the Classics Department at the University of Arizona helped make some sense of the corrupt Latin phrases recorded in the manuscript. The Southwestern Mission Research Center at the University of Arizona paid for the photographic illustrations.

I am particularly indebted to my friend Jorge Olvera. Jorge not only checked my translation from the Spanish, but agonized with me over the meaning of many descriptions that were particularly obscure because the accompanying illustrations had not survived. There are likely to be some who disagree with my interpretations, but they are free to render their own versions from the Spanish transcript.

MARDITH K. SCHUETZ

Architectural Practice
in Mexico City

Introduction

"New aspects of the profession are taught here," declares the anonymous author of *Architectural Practice in Mexico City*. Although we may question his boast, he nevertheless has left us with unique insights into the profession that are as valuable to the study of the social and economic history of the Mexican colonial period as they are to the study of architectural history. But even if that were insufficient reason to catch our attention, the very rarity of such writings pertaining to architectural practices in New Spain should be. This is a one-of-a-kind manuscript. Until it surfaced, the seventeenth-century architectural treatise of Andrés de San Miguel, the Spanish-born Carmelite friar who practiced architecture in New Spain, was thought to be the only one produced in the New World. The impressive scholarship of Mexican art and architectural historians until now has been based on the chronicles and inspection accounts written by bishops and other clerics, whose orders built many of the colonial churches, and on building contracts and reports found in the records of churches and cathedrals and in the Archivo General de las Indias and the Archivo General de la Nación. Another body of data, that pertaining to guild ordinances dating back to the sixteenth century, has provided insight into the organization and workings of the trades. Those rich sources have helped historians assemble the building chronologies of Mexico's monumental structures, and sometimes those sources have provided data on the artisans involved in those building efforts. The treatises of Fray Andrés and our anonymous author present new dimensions for study. Fray Andrés's work, written in the second quarter of the seventeenth century, is very much a product of its time, exhibiting a kinship with the treatises of European architectural masters of the Renaissance. The work introduced here for the first time was written as a manual for the journeyman preparing for his master's examination. Penned some one hundred fifty years after Andrés's work, this manual reflects the rapid changes occurring in the profession as western countries plunged into the industrial age. It is more a personal account than an abstract handling of the theoretical and technical aspects of the profession. Something of the personality and character of the author are revealed in his writing.

The author intrigues us. Operating upon the assumption that he might have been well known in his time, his handwriting was compared with that in archival documents written by architects known to have worked in the eighteenth century. Unfortunately, his identity eludes us. There is a kind of brashness and pedantry in his writing: "The proper term is *cenefa*, not *zanefa*, as many improperly refer to it." We can picture him presenting his disposition before a court, hoping to impress the judges with his bad Latin. His pride in himself and in his profession is evident throughout the work, and we are left with the suspicion that he might have been a *criollo* (a native of Mexico born of pure Spanish ancestry) with a bit of a chip on his shoulder. That is suggested by his somewhat sarcastic remarks about the inferior status of the *maestro mayor* of the Royal Works in Mexico City in comparison with the status of the maestro mayor of Madrid.[1] His treatise is a rambling, unorganized mass of fascinating information that bears signs of having been written over a period of time as new thoughts occurred to him. Near the end of the manuscript, he wrote the heading "Convents with Water Grants" but forgot to follow it with any text on the subject. The manuscript ends abruptly

---

1. A *maestro mayor* was an architect in charge of a category of buildings, in this case the buildings that belonged to the crown, such as the palace and the cathedral.

with a brief list of technical terms that the author apparently forgot to include earlier. Was it his intention to reorganize his material in a more orderly fashion before publishing it? Did he fail to put his name on his manuscript because it was unfinished? His identity has been lost, but his contribution adds significantly to our knowledge of colonial building practices.

Internal evidence suggests that *Architectural Practice in Mexico City* was written between 1794 and 1813. With the exception of Fray Lorenzo de San Nicolás, the author mentions none of the Renaissance builders who had been so influential in previous centuries.[2] And although Fray Lorenzo presented résumés of the teachings of the great architects of his period, the author recommends Fray Lorenzo for his elucidation of Tomás Tosca's treatise on geometry and for his explanation of the technical terms of the profession.[3] The only other book on architecture he lists was one by "Uvolfio." If I am correct in identifying "Uvolfio" as John Woolfe, the coauthor of two volumes of the *Vitruvius Britannicus* published in 1767 and 1771, then our author's emphasis on building design was that reflected in the British survey of Palladianism, which was then popular.[4] The last date that can be pinpointed in the manuscript is 1794, the last year of the reign of the Conde de Revillagigedo, the second viceroy by that name who served from 1789 to 1794.[5] The manual could not have been written after 1813 because that was the year for the decree handed down by the Cortés de Cádiz which broke the control of the guilds by declaring that all men were free to engage in any trade without being licensed by a guild. Clearly that had not yet occurred when this manual was written.

2. Fray Lorenzo de San Nicolás, a Spanish architect, published books on architecture and mathematics in the seventeenth century. For more information, see Eugenio Llaguno y Amerola, *Noticias de los arquitectos y architectura desde su restauración* (Madrid: Imprenta Real, 1829), 4:20–26.

3. Father Tomás Vicente Tosca was a Spanish architect, mathematician, and philosopher who published books on these subjects in the late seventeenth and early eighteenth centuries. See Llaguno y Amerola, *Noticias de los arquitectos,* 4:102.

4. John Woolfe and James Gandon, *The British Architect: Containing Plans, Elevations, and Sections; of the Regular Buildings Both Public and Private in Great Britain,* vols. 4 and 5 of *Vitruvius Britannicus* (1767–1771; reprint, New York: Benjamin Blom, Inc., 1967).

5. Manuel Rivera Cambas, ed., *Los gobernantes de México* (1873; reprint, Mexico City: Joaquín Porrua, S.A., 1981).

Since this manual probably was written between 1794 and 1813, it is appropriate to include a brief description of Mexico City at that time. Mexico City was already a large metropolis in 1792 with a population of 120,602 that grew to 137,000 by 1804. It was laid out in prescribed Spanish fashion on a grid system oriented to the cardinal directions. Blocks of private residences and shops were interrupted by plazas, each of which was generally dominated by a church on one side. Certain streets, such as Plateros, San Francisco, Mirador de la Alameda, Santa Teresa, and Cordobanes, were wide enough to accommodate ten horsemen abreast. Most houses in the central portion of the city were made of stone and mortar, while modest dwellings of adobe and *carrizo* (cane) were typical of outlying *barrios*. Water was carried into the city through two aqueducts with outlets into public and private fountains, public offices, and baths. Water was also distributed door to door by vendors. It was a city with a wealth of fine buildings attesting to the taste and craftsmanship of three centuries of builders. The flamboyant churrigueresque, or ultra-baroque, style that had dominated eighteenth-century church construction was being swept aside for a return to the quieter order of neo-classicism. For all its ostentatious wealth and extravagance, Mexico City was also unbelievably filthy and crime-ridden until the concerted efforts of Viceroy Revillagigedo, who sought to reverse the blight, began to pay off in the early 1790s. The main streets were paved and lighting installed. Police protection was boosted, and new ordinances were passed to clean up the water supply. Many of the sewers and canals, vestiges of Aztec times, were covered. And new markets were established so that the vendors, who had cluttered the great central plaza, had other places in which to hawk their wares.[6]

Against this backdrop we can imagine the movements of the various builders. The maestro of the Royal Works divides his time between the cathedral, where final construction of the towers is underway, and the Royal Palace, where the viceroy's wife is demanding that her drawing room be repainted. The maestro of Mexico City has his hands more than full as he moves from one job to another: inspecting a recent caulking job on the reservoir to see if the

6. Manuel Carrera Stampa, *Planos de la Ciudad de México,* Boletín de la Sociedad Mexicana de Geografía y Estadística, vol. 67, nos. 2–3 (Mexico City, 1949), 245.

leaks have been stopped, racing with Indians to put out a fire, and making repairs on one of the vendor's stalls in the plaza. Carts noisily creak into the city carrying beams and planks for a construction job. A journeyman at a construction site orders sand and lime from respective vendors and then checks the pilings to be sure they are ready for the mortar to complete the foundation. The maestro of one of the convents completes his estimate of repairs to a kitchen and assures the majordomo of the convent that the cost is trifling. The day wears on in our imagination, and we can see the involvement of the maestro, the journeyman (apprentice architect), the mason, and the stonecutter through the peephole offered by this manual.

Although much of the book retraces familiar ground, there also is new information. The author's discussion of building materials, though not new, does give us data on their origin or manufacture, their grades and prices, and how they were sold (such as by the *braza* or the *viage*). His directions for mixing mortars, whitewashes, and pitch are of interest to restoration architects today who are returning to the use of old materials as they find that modern compounds are incompatible with stone and adobe construction. The manuscript provides us with an enlightening lexicon of technical terms. Some may have been colloquialisms; others are now obsolete or are used with different meanings. Their late eighteenth-century usage provides us with clues to the changes in language that have occurred in the last two hundred years and which can be used to build up a series of meanings for a clearer understanding of those terms. These aspects of the work, although not as well organized for ready retrieval, are closer to the eighteenth-century *Builder's Dictionary* than to earlier Renaissance books on architecture.[7]

Perhaps the greatest contribution of this architect's manual is the light it sheds on the state of the profession in New Spain at the end of the colonial period. Unlike in England and most European countries, the profession was still controlled by the guild. Some of the information the author included reflects ordinances passed by the guilds in 1599 and 1736. For example, the examination taken by the journeyman to obtain his master's license was known to cover geometry and arithmetic (the latter for the computation of areas and

---

7. *The Builder's Dictionary: or Gentleman and Architect's Companion* (1734; reprint, Washington: Association for Preservation Technology, 1981).

masses), the construction of all types of arches and the proper manner of buttressing them, the thickness of walls required for certain
buildings, the construction of chimneys and staircases, laying tile,
mixing mortars, the proper proportions for portals, the healthful
siting of a structure, and more. He mentions some of these points
in the context of his description of the examination; other points,
such as calculating masses or areas, he covers in considerable detail
so that the new maestro will be well instructed in making appraisals.
He even includes a street-by-street inventory of sites in the city with
their evaluations. It will be of some interest to scholars of the devel-
opment of Mexico City to find that more dams are listed than had
previously been known. Many of the ordinances relate to the structure and officers of the guild and to the organization of the *cofradía*
(religious brotherhood), which are scarcely touched upon here.[8] In
this manuscript the author writes that there were two classifications
of licensed practitioners in the guild to which architects, masons,
and stonecutters belonged. Art historians have known that these cat-
egories of *de lo blanco* (white) and *de lo prieto* (black) were used in
the Guild of Carpenters, Joiners, Sculptors, and Instrument Makers.
Those with more advanced skills, who made retables or *mudéjar* ceilings, were *de lo blanco,* while ordinary carpenters were *de lo prieto.*
An equivalent distinction in the Guild of Architects has until now
been unknown. Maestros who had been examined *de lo prieto* were
limited to constructions of adobe and prohibited from making appraisals. The author also reveals other changes in the guild since the
1736 ordinances had been drawn up. One might attain the status of
maestro by being examined solely for one's knowledge of geometry
and arithmetic without being required to work as an apprentice and
journeyman.

Of particular interest are the author's several discussions of the
social and economic aspects of the profession. He familiarizes us
with the separate responsibilities of the maestro mayor of the Royal
Palace and the maestro mayor of Mexico City and notes their in-

8. For a description of earlier ordinances, see Manuel Carrera Stampa, *Los gremios mexicanos* (Mexico City: Ibero-Americana de Publicaciónes, 1954); or Barrio
Lorenzot, *Ordenanzas de gremios de la Nueva España* (Mexico City: Talleres Gráficos,
1920). A summary of the 1736 ordinances of the architect and mason's guild can be
found in Manuel Toussaint, *Colonial Art in Mexico* (Austin: University of Texas Press,
1967), 277–78.

ferior status in comparison with the maestro mayor of the Royal
Works in Madrid. He complains about the abuses and hazards of the
craft, such as the difficulty of collecting fees, and about bigotry
within the guild. He advises the new maestro on the proper manner
in which to address his workmen. He enumerates the ranks of masons, their helpers, and their salaries, and he informs us that payday
was Saturday and that one *real* a week was withheld for meals.

This manuscript is unique not only for what it covers but also
for what it does not cover. The author does not consider theory,
history, and style. Although he notes the accepted proportions for
rooms and churches, he offers no drawings of dignified buildings to
serve as guides, nor does he illustrate the classic orders, even though
a revival of classicism was underway. His drawings, now lost, apparently pertained to the prosaic: designing doors and raising walls. He
rather offhandedly suggests that the maestro should subcontract the
designing of an elegant portal to a master joiner. He informs us that
the walls of shops that sell pigs are infested with lice. Elsewhere he
states, "I have heard it said that a church should be oriented in such
a way that the principal door looks toward the west, to satisfy some
rite of the church that I do not understand." Unlike his predecessors,
this author feels no need to balance early cosmological considerations of architecture with practice. For our author the compulsion
to justify the design of a church as a revelation of a larger scheme of
the Creator has given way to a more secularized view of building,
one imposed by a new age and a new philosophy that would soon
be manifested in the industrial revolution. He has made the transi-
tion from the Renaissance to the modern age and is more concerned
with the mundane aspects of the trade.

Since the author states that he is setting forth "new aspects of
the profession," it is appropriate to examine a few works that pre-
ceded and were contemporary to his in order to assess his claim. In
his manuscript there is not a single reference to Vitruvius or to any
of the great builders of the Italian Renaissance. This is a strange
omission since surveys of colonial libraries by modern historians pa-
rade the names of both Italian and Spanish architects whose genius
for design was manifested on paper as well as in stone: Alberti, Serlio, Vignola, Barrocio, Palladio, Gamuzi, Cataneo, Potey, Arfe y Vi-
llafañe, López Arenas, Torija, Sagredo, Fernández de Medrano, San

Nicolás, and Tosca.[9] The influence that some of these European masters had on the designing of colonial buildings has been demonstrated repeatedly by architectural historians. From this manuscript, however, we might assume that only the Spanish masters San Nicolás and Tosca were known to our author, yet he must have had at least a nodding acquaintance with some of the others.

The model for all the Renaissance treatises on architecture was *The Ten Books on Architecture* by the Roman builder Marcus Vitruvius Pollio.[10] Written as a guide to building in the time of the Caesars, it survived in several editions throughout the Middle Ages and was rediscovered by Fra Giocondo, who introduced it to the Renaissance world with his publication of the ancient work in 1511. It was the catalyst to the Greco-Roman forms adopted and modified by builders during the ensuing three centuries.

In book 1 Vitruvius sets forth the educational qualifications for the architect, who should balance scholarship with manual skills: "Let him be educated, skillful with the pencil, instructed in geometry, know much history, have followed the philosophers with attention, understand music, have some knowledge of medicine, know the opinions of jurists, and be acquainted with astronomy and the theory of the heavens."[11] Book 1 covers the fundamental principles of the art—order, arrangement, eurythmy, symmetry, propriety, and economy—and the divisions of architecture—the art of building, making timepieces, the construction of machinery, and city planning.

Book 2, after speculating on the origin of houses, gets down to the nuts and bolts of the profession, describing building materials (brick, sand, lime, stone, and timber) and where they are found, how they are made, and their qualities and sizes, as well as methods of building walls.

9. For a survey of published works that found their way to the New World, see José Torre Revello, "Tratados de arquitectura utilizados en Hispanoamérica (Siglos XVI a XVII)," *Revista Interamericana de Bibliografía* 6 no. 1 (1956): 5–23; and María del Carmen Olvera C., "La biblioteca de un arquitecto de la virreinal en México," *Monumentos Históricos,* no. 6 (1981): 33–40.

10. Marcus Vitruvius Pollio, *Vitruvius: The Ten Books on Architecture* (ca. 27 B.C.; reprint, New York: Dover Publications, 1960).

11. Vitruvius, *Ten Books,* 5–6.

Books 3 and 4 deal with the symmetry of temples and the human body; the classification of temples, their orientation, and their proportions; and the classic orders.

Book 5 discusses public buildings and waterfront constructions.

In book 6 Vitruvius writes about private residences, climatic considerations, the propriety of rooms and their suitable measurements, foundations, and substructures.

Vitruvius returns to mechanics in book 7: floors, slaking lime for stucco, vaulting, pigments, decorating dining rooms, and the decadence of fresco painting. Book 8 discusses water: the properties of different waters, tests for good water, leveling and leveling instruments, aqueducts, wells, and cisterns.

The zodiac and astrology, astronomical observations, the analemma and its applications, sundials, water clocks, and weather prognostication are considered in book 9. The concluding book discusses hydraulic devices and military machines such as catapults and ballistae.

Leone Battista Alberti, whose first edition in Latin of *Ten Books on Architecture* was published in 1485, followed Vitruvius's lead by organizing his material into the same number of books and maintaining a balance between scholarship and mechanics.[12] All types of ecclesiastical, public, and private construction are considered. City planning, the classic orders, and climatic factors are given their due, all illustrated with historic examples and, in some cases, outright myths: "The Water of Diana's Fountain, near *Camerinum,* will mix with nothing Male. . . . In *Eleufina* near *Athens,* is a spring which leaps and rejoices at the sound of a Flute. Foreign Animals that drink at the River *Indus,* change their colour. . . ."[13]

Alberti, too, deals with the technical aspects of foundations and wall construction, tools for moving heavy materials, and building materials themselves. However, his discourses also reveal the Renaissance fascination with the significance of numbers, numerical proportions, and astrology. There are proper seasons not only for beginning and finishing buildings, but also for collecting materials:

12. Leone Battista Alberti, *Ten Books on Architecture* (1755; reprint, London: Alec Tirante, Ltd., 1955).

13. Alberti, *Ten Books,* 213.

". . . such Things as are destined in their Uses to be moveable, ought to be cut and wrought when the Moon is in *Libra* or *Cancer;* but such as are to be fixed and immoveable, when she is in *Leo, Taurus,* or the like. But that timber ought to be cut in the Wane of the Moon, all the Learned agree, because they hold that the flegmatick Moisture, so very liable to immediate Putrefaction, is then almost quite dried up, and it is certain, that when it is cut in such a Moon, it is never apt to breed worms."[14]

Sebastiano Serlio's *The Five Books of Architecture* were originally published as separate books between 1537 and 1547 and finally put together as a single work in 1584.[15] Books 1 and 2 deal with geometry and perspective, respectively. Temples, theaters, obelisks, bridges, and triumphal arches of antiquity are covered in book 3. Books 4 and 5 deal with the five classic orders, their uses, diverse forms of temples, symmetry, and ways to lay brick. Again the proper obeisance to historical precedents and Vitruvius are observed.

Within a decade after Serlio's work became available as a single publication, Andrea Palladio's *The Four Books of Architecture* appeared in 1570.[16] The first book discusses building materials; foundations; the construction of roofs, walls, chimneys, and stairs; the classic orders; the proper proportions for different spaces; types of vaults; door and window dimensions; and ornaments. The second and third books deal with private residences and public buildings (both Greek and Roman), respectively. The final book is devoted entirely to Roman temples, with the exception of a single design by the Italian Renaissance architect and painter Bramante. Palladio, too, frequently refers to Vitruvius, and the influence of Serlio is obvious in Palladio's designs.

In the seventeenth century the Spanish Carmelite friar Andrés de San Miguel left numerous writings based upon years of research and experience as a master of architecture and carpentry in New Spain. His treatises, which were written in the 1640s, remained unpublished until this century and were probably unknown to our

14. Alberti, *Ten Books,* 26.
15. Sebastiano Serlio, *The Five Books of Architecture* (1611; reprint, New York: Dover Publications, Inc., 1982).
16. Andrea Palladio, *The Four Books of Architecture* (1738; reprint, New York: Dover Publications, Inc., 1965).

maestro, but they are pertinent as a link between the philosophical views of architects in the sixteenth and eighteenth centuries.[17] Fray Andrés's work is organized by chapters and dispenses with divisions into books. Again we find the concern with both historical perspective and practical experience, but there are some singularly Spanish and colonial interests that distinguish it from the writings of the Italian masters. Along with the Temple of Solomon, he describes Peruvian temples. In addition to the usual lessons of geometry he discusses its application to the design of Moorish *alfarje* ceilings. His indebtedness to others is acknowledged, for his discussions of foundations and the thicknesses and heights of walls are drawn from Vitruvius and Alberti. In Fray Andrés's book the hold of Renaissance cosmography is still strong, and he outlines his reasons for believing that the heavens are as solid as the earth and that there are eleven heavens.

In England an entirely new philosophy of architecture was signaled by the appearance of the builder's dictionary. In the preface to a reprint of *The Builder's Dictionary: or Gentleman and Architect's Companion*, it is stated that: "The harbinger of the builder's lexicon may have been Joseph Moxon's *Mechanick Exercises* published serially starting in 1670, written to demystify various crafts, including the building trades, which had been cloaked in guild secrecy. The inclusion of a glossary of terms, as in the 1703 edition of Moxon, may have been the beginning of an architectural dictionary."[18]

The Builder's Dictionary, which was first published in 1734, provides an example of the fully developed guide to building. Its scope is indicated on its title page:

Explaining not only the Terms of Art in all the several Parts of Architecture, But also containing the Theory and Practice of the Various Branches thereof, requisite to be known by Masons, Carpenters, Joiners, Bricklayers, Plaisterers, Painters, Glaziers, Smiths, Turners, Carvers, Statuaries, Plumbers, etc. Also Necessary Problems in Arithmetic, Geometry, Mechanics, Perspective, Hydraulics, and other Mathematical Sciences. To-

17. Andrés de San Miguel, *Obras de Fray Andrés de San Miguel* (Mexico City: Universidad Nacional Autónoma de México, 1969).

18. *The Builder's Dictionary*, iii.

gether with The Quantities, Proportions, and Prices of all Kinds of Materials used in Building; with Directions for Chusing, Preparing, and Using them: The several proportions of the Five Orders of Architecture, and all their Members, according to Vitruvius, Palladio, Scamozzi, Vignola, M. Le Clerc, etc. With Rules for the Valuation of Houses, and Expense calculated of Erecting any Fabrick Great or Small.[19]

The entries run from "abacus" to "zoophorick column." The approach is down-to-earth. The old lessons are combined with such practical concerns as building costs. Under "Tileing" we learn that ". . . for Workmanship only, they reckon at London, 5 s. per Square; but in the Country, the Price is various."[20] Under "Stone" we find an aside which reminds us of the author of this manual: "As to the Price of scapting Stones. Some reckon 5 s. the 100 Foot, this they say, is Journey-man's Wages, out of which the Master has but a small Profit. . . ."[21] An important point is made in the title. The book has been prepared for the gentleman builder, as well as for the architect, to serve as a guide so that he can oversee construction and calculate the costs himself. Building is no longer the sole province of the professional in some parts of the world.

Such how-to manuals proliferated in the nineteenth century. Asher Benjamin's *The American Builder's Companion or, a System of Architecture Particularly Adapted to the Present Style of Building* is illustrative of the trend.[22] The first edition, which appeared in 1806, included a number of designs inspired by Charles Bulfinch in the Federal Style, or the American adaptations of such English builders as Robert and James Adam or James Gibbs. The book is arranged as a series of illustrations with explanations or directions for each figure. Some show geometric forms and their application to columns, moldings, and the classic orders. There are designs for doors, sashes, windows, staircases, bannisters, rails, ornaments, roof trusses, and chimneys. Other plates offer plans and elevations for town and coun-

19. *The Builder's Dictionary,* v.
20. *The Builder's Dictionary,* s.v. "tileing."
21. *The Builder's Dictionary,* s.v. "stone."
22. Asher Benjamin, *The American Builder's Companion or, a System of Architecture Particularly Adapted to the Present Style of Building* (1827; reprint, New York: Dover Publications, Inc., 1969).

try houses, churches, a courthouse, and a kitchen fireplace. There are also written guidelines to assure a pleasing aspect: "openings of windows and doors in different stories, ought to be exactly perpendicular one over the other."[23]

In regard to building practices, the author of *Architectural Practice in Mexico City* mentions only three architects. He refers to Fray Lorenzo de San Nicolás and his test for the best sand with which to make mortar. If he had no book in his library other than that of this seventeenth-century architect, the author still would have had some exposure to the Italian Renaissance masters, for Fray Lorenzo provided résumés of their techniques. A copy of the friar's book is one of three on architecture that the author recommends for the new maestro.

The second book the author recommends is the treatise of Tomás Tosca. The author compares the two: "A set of Father Laurencio's [Lorenzo's] writings on architecture which, in comparison to Father Tosca's shorter treatise, is not as good, but nevertheless sheds much light on understanding it [Tosca's] and presenting other information, above all in teaching the terms and material language of the maestros." The author drew on Tosca in his own manual, copying almost verbatim Tosca's short section on the terminology of the stonecutter. *Tratados de arquitectura civil, montea y cantería y reloxes* was published in 1694.[24] It is divided into two treatises, the first covering civil architecture: the five orders, proportions of churches and residences, and ichnographic, profile, and perspective drawings. The second treatise on designing and cutting stone outlines fundamental principles of the art (including definitions of terms, tools, and stonecutting) and the various kinds of arches and vaults.

The third source the author recommends is the mysterious "Uvolfio" because "what he wrote on architecture is so special that one should not want any other subject matter." It is likely that Uvolfio was John Woolfe, the coauthor with James Gandon of volumes 4 and 5 of the *Vitruvius Britannicus,* published in 1767 and 1771.[25] These volumes consist of nothing more than plates showing the

23. Benjamin, *Builder's Companion,* 109.
24. Tosca, Tomás Vicente, *Tratados de arquitectura civil, montea y cantería y reloxes* (Valencia: Oficina de los Hermanos de Orga, 1694).
25. Woolfe and Gandon, *The British Architect.*

plans and elevations of private residences of the English gentry. The designs—with their symmetrical arrangements incorporating the classic orders and such Renaissance innovations as the use of rusticated stone on lower courses and quoins, balustrades, domes and cupolas, sashes, doors with Gibbs surrounds, and "Palladian" windows (or, more properly, Serliana)—are indicative of the enthusiasm with which the English adopted Palladianism when Inigo Jones introduced the style in the seventeenth century. The plates are accompanied by short descriptions, such as this one:

> Thorseby Lodge is the seat of his grace the duke of Kingston in Nottinghamshire: He erected this elegant villa in 1768, upon one of the most delightful spots in the kingdom. The ascent to the principal story of the house, is by a double stair-case within the base story, that terminates in an eleptical-hall in the center of the house, and which leads to all the apartments upon the principal and attic floors. They are conveniently disposed to suit the situation, and are handsomely furnished. The principal front is ornamented with a tetrastyle portico of the Ionick order, of a beautiful stone upon a rustic basement, and the other fronts are regularly decorated. This design was made by Mr. Carr of York, to whom we are obliged for these drawings. . . .[26]

If I am right in my identification of Uvolfio, then the classic revivalism of Palladianism is the only clue the author leaves as to his own preference in style. This assumption does accord with the turn-of-the-century change in Mexico from the ultra-baroque to classic revivalism.

One statement made by the author of this manual, however, could make the equation of Woolfe with Uvolfio a risky one. He notes that "he [Uvolfio] wrote on the mixture of mortars and other skills not to be found in any other author," yet the Woolfe and Gandon volumes are strictly design books. But the difficulty in identifying any other architect with a name resembling Uvolfio who practiced in this time period emboldens me to suggest an explanation for this contradiction. If one assumes that the author might have been writing from memory, it is reasonable to surmise that he

26. Woolfe and Gandon, *The British Architect*, 5:3.

may well have confused Woolfe with Palladio, given the similarity of the two architects' work in terms of architectural style. Palladio's mortar formula of two parts of sea or river sand to one part of lime is the same as the author's *mescla segunda,* although it should be noted that both are presumably derived from Vitruvius.[27]

Several characteristics of this manuscript should be noted here. The manuscript is written in a clear, easily read script which made it possible, for the most part, to work from a photocopy when translating. There were only a handful of words which were too faded to reproduce clearly, and this difficulty was overcome by the loan of the document from the owner so that the original might be consulted. Upon completion of the transcription the book was returned to its owner. There is no microfilm copy available and the manuscript is not available for examination by the public.

The illustrations described by the anonymous author are missing from the manuscript. In only two instances was I successful at reconstructing the drawings. The other illustrations were selected to show monumental structures built under one of the maestros mayores described by the author or plans for buildings drawn by an architect of the same period.

No attempt was made to render the original text into modern Spanish. The author's orthography, repeated words, punctuation, coupled words, and syntax have, with a few exceptions, been retained, no matter how obscure, in order to preserve the idiosyncrasies of his writing and to avoid errors of interpretation. However, abbreviations, such as "xpna" (*cristiana*) and "dho" (*dicho*), and superscripted abbreviations have been spelled out. Paragraphs are indented, the beginning letters of sentences have been capitalized, and periods have been added at the end of sentences. Bracketed additions to some sentences have been made to clarify the meaning. The author systematically misspelled *ciudad,* rendering it *"cuidad,"* an error that has been corrected to avoid confusion. In the translation, modern spellings of place names have been substituted for the author's idiosyncratic spellings. Many technical terms have not been translated, either because they have a more specific interpretation than translation allows or because their eighteenth-century meanings dif-

27. Vitruvius, *Ten Books,* 45.

fer from contemporary usage. These terms are explained both in the footnotes and the glossary. In many cases the author was inconsistent in his spelling, which is not unusual in colonial manuscripts. What is a bit out of the ordinary is his spelling of such words as *architectura* or *arquitetura* (usually spelled *arquitectura*); *mechanica* (*mecánica*), *authores* (*autores*), and *cathedral* (*catedral*). Such Latin and European influences are indicative of an educated writer accustomed to reading other languages. Since he is not consistent in the spelling of some of these words, it was likely an unconscious rather than a pedantic impulse.

A blank front page of the book contains a cartoon added in a hand other than that of the manual's author that was certainly written at a later date. The cartoon depicts two figures. One is a man holding a saber in one hand and an umbrella in the other, dressed in an oriental-looking tunic, with a high neck and wide sleeves, over a pair of long trousers. The other is a woman carrying a jug in one hand and a jar in the other, dressed in a long-sleeve blouse and pinafore. Written above the figures is the inscription, "Este libro es de Manuel Barona" (this book belongs to Manuel Barona). Emanating from the mouth of the male figure is the quotation, "y yo que soi Manuel Barona digo que soi el dueño del Libro Migas y Borrachera" (and I who am Manuel Barona declare that I am the owner of this book of *migas* and drunkenness). Coming from the mouth of the female figure is the quotation, "María Manuela de Soria llebo las Migas para los Pobez y la borrachera" (María Manuela de Soria carried the *migas* for the poor and the drunks). Off to one side is the profile bust of a male figure attired in a uniform with a high collar, buttoned across the shoulder and down one side. Might he represent a fencing opponent? *Migas* is a type of soup made with bread crumbs that is considered efficacious for hangovers. Efforts to identify Barona and his wife were unsuccessful.

An eighteenth-century architect (left) in the midst of his work. (*The Build-er's Dictionary: or Gentleman and Architect's Companion,* 1734.)

Architectural Practice in Mexico City

Author's Declaration

In books of architecture, as one will see in the context of this writing and its paragraphs, even though some points of geometry are touched upon, it is only insofar as they teach the method of applying them to practice, and this is very distinct from the way such matters are treated in the books. New aspects of the profession are taught here which, up until now perhaps, have not been written. These have been made at the expenditure of great effort in collecting the latest information on aspects touching upon sites and prices, for whose true and current evaluation the maestro will refer to the schedule and custom of his time and place. From the terms used by the political government, the profession, and vulgar terminology from the mouths of the workmen, and without neglecting from time to time to introduce certain juridicial points when they are important, the maestro will be able to give a legitimate declaration before any court.

In everything I recognize the authority of Christian discipline and the amendment and teaching of whatever may be my skill (even though I may not boast of it out of humility, or because I do not have to).

What is Treated Here Is Not to Be Found in
Books on Mathematics Terms, Government, and Application
[of the Profession]

Floors. The starting point for a building is the floor. Its value is measured in square *varas*,[1] and each vara has a price dependent upon the geographic area which updates the schedule of prices drawn up long ago by a *junta de cabildo* in the time of the *regidor* Don Antonio Dávalos.[2]

Maestros mayores of this profession are the titles bestowed upon mayores respective to the public work with which they are charged, for example, "Don So-and-So, Master of the Royal Buildings, of the State, the Holy Office,[3] etc." In the city there is a maestro mayor, of whom I shall treat later, who is charged with everything related to city works, including the four quadrants, freight system, pipelines, and works of the Royal Drainage Ditch of Huehuetoca. The maestro mayor of the Royal Palace receives his annual salary from His Majesty and has in his charge the buildings belonging to the king.

Foundations and trenches. We do not take churches into consideration here because the stresses of such buildings must be calculated according to specialists. We speak, then, of ordinary houses with their stories and mezzanines. The usual foundation is a vara wide and a vara and a half deep, or two varas beneath the datum line.

Heights and thicknesses of walls. From the top of the footing to the level of the first roof the wall is three-fourths vara thick, and from that point to the top, two-thirds or one-half vara. *Accesorios* or *zaguanes* are five varas high, mezzanines three varas, the height upstairs six.[4] If no mezzanine is built the downstairs is six-and-a-half varas and the upstairs six. All this is arbitrary.

1. The *vara* was a unit of measurement, roughly equivalent to three feet, although it varied slightly from region to region. It was calibrated into halves, thirds, fourths, sixths, eighths, and *dedos* ("fingers," which measured approximately one-half inch).

2. One of the duties of the *cabildo,* or municipal government, was to regulate prices, including those for materials and craftsmen's services. A *junta de cabildo* was a meeting of the government.

3. Holy Office of the Inquisition.

4. *Accesorios* were lower-level shops that opened onto the street. A *zaguán* was an entryway, located in the center of a facade, of sufficient width and height to admit horses and carriages into the patio.

Partitions [non–load-bearing walls]. Those downstairs are one-half vara; those upstairs one third. This is the norm, but according to Alemán, it might be reduced to one fourth.[5]

Staking the site.[6] After outlining the foundation with powdered lime, the trench is opened, leveled, and straightened with a mason's square and lines. All this is done according to the owner of the building, because the stakes might be very close together or more widely separated. The cost of the stakes depends upon the locale. If four stakes are made from a pole they pay 5 reales per hundred. Each cartload carries twenty-five poles. Each one, which is six varas long, is worth 1½ reales apart from the transportation cost. Sharpening these can be arranged with the carpenter on the job.

Trenches for staking. The foundation for anything is called a *cepa*.[7] For whatever construction the foundation trench is opened for three or four varas, conforming to the ground and the size and shape of the structure, with the warning that the stakes have to be contiguous. Later hard stone with mortar is poured to within one vara of grade. The remaining vara or vara and a half is for filling and leveling to grade with hard stone and *tezontlale*, or fine mortar.[8]

Sand is hauled by burros or mules, each burro carrying twelve to sixteen sacks, or each mule three to four sacks. According to Father Laurencio,[9] the best is that which, spilled on your clothes, leaves

5. This may refer to Marco Aurelio Alemán, a mathematician who in 1552 published his *Libro primero de aritmética alebraica*. He may have illustrated the book with architectural examples. See *Diccionario enciclopédico UTEHA* (Mexico City: Unión Tipográfica, Editorial Hispano-Americana, 1950–64).

6. To stake a site was to place wooden pilings under the footings that were necessary in the marshy terrain of Mexico City. This was an ancient technique, described by Vitruvius, the Roman builder. He wrote that when building on unconsolidated soils, the foundations "must be dug up and cleared out and set with piles made of charred alder or olive wood or oak, and these must be driven down by machinery, very closely together like bridge piles, and the intervals between them filled in with charcoal, and finally the foundations are to be laid on them in the most solid form of construction." (Marcus Vitruvius Pollio, *Vitruvius: The Ten Books on Architecture*, trans. Morris Hicky Morgan [New York: Dover Publications, 1960], 88.)

7. A *cepa* (or *zepa*) is the hole excavated for the foundation of a structure.

8. *Tezontlale* is a mortar made from the volcanic rock *tezontle*. The author of the manuscript also spelled these words *tezonclale* and *tesoncle* (or *tezoncle*). The various spellings have been regularized in the translation.

9. Fray Lorenzo (also spelled Laurencio in the text) de San Nicolás was born in Madrid in the 1590s. The first part of his *Arte y uso de la arquitectura*, published in 1633, brought together the principles of arithmetic and geometry and the theory and

no dust; and according to others, it is that which, rubbed between the hands, leaves no clay. It comes from various places, such as La Piedad, Tacubaya, Escapusalco, etc.[10] The cost is calculated by the load, and a load of sand corresponds to the box in which it is put.[11] Eight boxes are worth 4 reales, though there are other loads which cost 5 reales for the same eight boxes.

Lime comes from various places. The best is that of San Marcos.[12] The superior grade makes much noise when slaked and makes the best whitewash. Lime corresponds to cartloads: a cartload has to have ten *cargas*[13] and each carga has to have twelve *arrobas*, twelve pounds.[14] From each carga twelve pounds are deducted as tare.

Mortars. *La real* is composed of one basket of lime to one of

---

practice of architecture. The second part, which was published in 1664, corrected errors in the first; presented the organization and dimensions of the classic orders; gave résumés of the teachings of Vitruvius and the Renaissance architects Serlio, Palladio, Vignola, Sagredo, Arfe, Viola, and Scamozi; offered short treatises on the works of Cataneo, Labaco, Alberti, and Busconi; and included translations of and commentaries on Euclid. In 1667 the first part was reprinted to include the translations of and commentaries on Euclid. Lorenzo's publications, aimed at a readership of apprentices, were considered of particular value to stonecutters and masons, which is confirmed by the author of this manual when he notes Lorenzo's value "in teaching the terms and material language of the maestro." Lorenzo was a working architect as well as a theoretician, and he built sixteen churches and chapels. He died in Madrid in 1679. See Eugenio Llaguno y Amerola, *Noticias de los arquitectos y arquitectura desde su restauración* (Madrid: En la Imprenta Real, 1829), 20–26.

10. The barrio of La Piedad was located southwest of the cathedral. Tacubaya was located southwest of Mexico City and of the Bosque de Chapultepec. Escapusalco was northwest of the city, near the river of the same name which fed into Lake Texcoco, and just north of Tacuba. These places are named on many eighteenth-century maps such as one by Don Carlos de Sigüenza that was amended by Don Joseph Antonio de Alzate y Ramirez and published in 1776. See map 54 in *Cartografía de ultramar. Carpeta III: Mexico* (Madrid: Imprenta del Servicio Geográfico del Ejército, 1955).

11. The word for load used by the author is *viage*, which in the eighteenth century meant the weight of one load carried from one place to another in a single trip. It was a variable unit.

12. The settlement of San Marcos was located southeast of Mexico City, on a road branching southeastward from the Camino de los Correos, which led to Puebla and Vera Cruz. See map 54 in *Cartografía de ultramar.*

13. A *carga* generally meant the weight that a man or beast could carry from one place to another. This manuscript suggests that for certain commodities, at least, the carga of a cartload had been standardized.

14. An *arroba* was a unit of weight equal to twenty-five pounds. Each cartload, which held twelve arrobas and twelve pounds, thus carried 3,120 pounds.

sand. *Mescla segunda* is made of one of lime to two of sand. *Mescla fina* has one part of lime to one of sifted sand. If one is left with a half box of siftings, one should mix it with a half box of lime. Mortar for plastering has one of sand to one of lime, mixed together first and then sifted. *Mescla terciada,* primarily for foundations, is composed of three boxes of lime, six of sand, and twelve of earth.[15]

Stone. To build of rubble the stone has to be hard and is measured in *brazas*. A braza is four varas long, two wide, and one deep.[16] The regular price is 4 pesos.

Tezontle is measured in the same way as hard stone. There are two qualities of this stone that come from Mexico: one from La Joya, which is hard, and one from La Barranca, which is soft.[17] The soft is worth 6 pesos per braza, the hard 5 pesos. There are *brazadas* of *tezontle* called *laja* and *media laja*.[18] The *media laja* is larger than the *laja*. The price of the *laja* and *media laja* is sometimes 8 pesos, sometimes 12 pesos.

Stone for faceting [stone which can be faceted into the dimensions given] is frequently divided into two qualities: *cantería* and *chiluca*. *Cantería* is less hard than *chiluca* and comes from Los Remedios and other places.[19] Each can be used as an *atravesado*[20] or as

15. The types of mortar described can be translated as royal grade (*la real*), second-quality (*mescla segunda*), and mortar made of three ingredients (*mescla terciada*). Roman mortar was three parts sand and one part lime, or two parts river or sea sand and one part lime. See Vitruvius, *Ten Books,* 45.

16. A *braza* of these dimensions contained eight square varas of stone.

17. La Joya is an area within La Pedregal, which is now a neighborhood of Mexico City located within a volcanic zone. The particular *barranca* (canyon) where the *tezontle* was quarried cannot be identified.

18. According to the author's definition of *braza*, a *brazada* of stone was eight square varas. The meanings of *laja* and *media laja* in relation to *tezontle* are obscure since *laja* refers to a flagstone or a slab derived from sedimentary rock. Equally mysterious is why a *media laja* was larger than a *laja*.

19. Los Remedios was located west of Mexico City between branches of the Río de Escapusalco, according to a map drawn by Don Juan Lopez in 1785. See map 56 in *Cartografía de ultramar.*

20. *Atravesados* were long stones used as window lintels. The dimensions presented by the author are somewhat smaller than those established in 1736 in the revised ordinances of the Guild of Masons and Architects. The 1736 specifications for *atravesado* were three-fourths vara long, one-half vara wide, and one-half vara thick. See Manuel Toussaint, *Colonial Art in Mexico* (Austin: University of Texas Press, 1967), 278.

an ashlar measuring two-thirds vara long by one-half vara wide by one-fourth vara, two dedos thick.[21] *Pisietes* of *cantería* or *chiluca* are one-half vara long, slightly over one-third vara wide, and one-fourth vara thick.[22] *Pisietes* are worth half the value of *atravesado*, each load of *atravesado* costing 3½ to 5 reales. There is another kind of stone that they call *colorada* [red] and comes only from Guadalupe.[23] *Guijarro* [cobbles] are hard, rounded stones that are brought solely from Tacubaya. The load is 5 reales for three sacks, the same as a load of sand.

A *ladrillo de marca* [first-quality brick in standard measurements] is one-third vara long, one-sixth vara wide, and three dedos thick. A *ladrillo común* [common brick] is three dedos thick and nearly one-third vara long and nearly one-sixth vara wide. The larger ones are from 5 pesos 4 reales to 6 pesos the thousand; the best are recognizable by their better firing. There are four grades of brick: refired, recolored, red, and orange. The first and second are of good quality, the latter two inferior. Good brick comes from Tacubaya, Los Morales, Mixcuaque, Piedad, etc.[24] A lesser quality comes from Mexico City, although it is good for rubble construction and other things.

Flagstones.[25] These are called *tenayucas* and measure up to a vara.[26] Their price is 1 real. But this is not standardized, since they also come in three-fourths, one-half, and one-third vara sizes.

Wood is used for all sorts of work. The principal species are fir,

21. A dedo was one forty-eighth of a Castillian vara, or approximately one-half inch.

22. *Pisietes* were faceted stones used in the construction of pilasters, according to the author. They were also probably used in constructing other structural elements such as columns.

23. The Sierra de Guadalupe, located west of Lake Texcoco and north of Mexico City.

24. Los Morales was located on a hill due west of Mexico City, according to a map drawn by Don Louis Martin in 1807. (Ola Apenas, *Mapas antiguos del valle de México* [Mexico City: Universidad Nacional Autonoma de México, Instituto de Historia, 1947], map 30.) By Mixcasaque the author meant the barrio of Mixcuaque, located south of Chapultepec. It appears on several eighteenth-century maps such as the 1763 map of Yldefonso de Yniesta Vejarano (map 51 in *Cartografía de ultramar*).

25. The word *loza*, used to mean flagstone in the text, should not be confused with the same word used to mean china or ceramic tile.

26. *Tenayucas* were mined in the settlement of the same name northwest of Mexico City.

royal pine, cedar, and torch pine. Beginning with those from Ista-paluca, it is said that they are at least six varas, three dedos thick and valued at 3 reales.[27] Then there are quarter-sawed timbers of fir of seven varas valued at 3½ reales. Quarter-sawed timbers of eight varas are 4 reales. Timbers for *antepechos* [railings or window sills] come in six varas and are either custom-cut or regular. Custom-cut [*antepechos*] are thicker. Beams come in seven-vara lengths and are valued at 7 reales. Those of eight varas are 8 reales (and these are either regular or custom-cut). Beams of nine varas are 9 to 10 reales. Beams of ten varas are from 12 to 14 reales (and these are custom-cut or regular). Beams of eleven varas are 2 pesos. Beams of twelve varas are 18 to 20 reales. The price, however, fluctuates on all these. Cedar planks, called *lumbrales,* are of five varas.[28] There are some others six varas in length by one-half vara in width by one-third vara in breadth which are sawed as planks. Most are fir, but they can be of royal pine, etc. Ordinarily each freight load is worth 4 reales and is billed to the owner of the work. A typical freight load from Istapaluca might carry sixteen quarter-sawed timbers of seven varas and eight quarter-sawed timbers of eight varas. Six beams at seven varas con-stitute a cartload, or four beams at eight varas and three beams at nine varas another. Two beams of eleven varas and one beam at twelve varas make another. One *lumbral* may be in each cart. Twenty-five cedar poles fit in one cart.

Ceiling boards and shingles are of three species: some of royal pine, which go for 2 reales a dozen, others of fir or *chalco* valued at 3 or 4 reales a dozen.[29] These are one-and-a-quarter varas long, one-third vara wide, and one dedo thick. Planks from Ixtlahuaca are two varas long, one-half vara wide, and one *pulgada* [inch] thick with a value of 8 to 12 reales a dozen.[30] Boards are placed on ceilings in two manners: closely joined or overlapping. In whichever manner

27. Ixtapaluca (Ystapaluca in the manuscript) was located southeast of Mexico City on the far side of Lake Texcoco and just north of the road to Puebla.

28. *Lumbrales* are lintels and doorsills, or wood planks cut for that purpose.

29. Chalco was an unidentified species of wood brought from the village of the same name located on the south bank of the Acequia Real de Chalco, southeast of Mexico City. See map 51 in *Cartografía de ultramar.*

30. San Mateo Ixtlahuaca (Ysclahuaca in the manuscript) was located northeast of Mexico City and south of Atotonilco, according to an 1828 map drawn by Don Tomás Ramón del Moral. See Apenas, *Mapas antiguos,* map 32.

they are placed, they require strips of shingles [to cover the seams to shed water]. There are 120 shingles to a load, with a value of 27 reales.

Iron for forging comes by the pound. The largest *barretas* edged in steel from end to end have to weigh nineteen pounds. Each wrought pound is worth 4 reales to the blacksmith or a sum agreed upon. *Azadones* are from five to six pounds but no heavier. The cost of the same when forged depends upon the blacksmith, and the same can be said of *rodadillos*. Iron is used for grills, windows, corridors, handrails, etc. If, according to the contract, the owner buys the iron and pays the blacksmith 7 or 8 pesos per hundredweight for ordinary work, any loss of material is charged to the blacksmith. If fine work is done, an adjustment is made in pounds. Manufactured half-orange nails for doors have a value of 2½ to 3 reales a dozen. Spikes are from 9 to 12 reales a dozen. These are regularly made in Xochimilco.[31] There are also hooks for padlocks, windows, and brackets that have to be custom-made, as well as such things as escutcheons, latches, etc.

Various Terms Used by Maestros

The *taller* [atelier] has become the shop where architects work. The principal one is the one who pays the others and is in the position of being the maestro and is called *capataz* [overseer].

The *tapial* is the wooden barricade enclosing a construction site so that the street remains open to passage. Construction materials are stored within.

Vertical lines on a wall have to be scribed with a plumb, and horizontal parallel lines with a level. A *cateto* is the perpendicular line which descends from top to bottom and no other.[32]

Michinales are the holes remaining from the scaffolding upon conclusion of construction.[33]

31. Half-orange nails were nails with semicircular heads, the equivalent of to-day's rose nail heads.

32. *Cateto* is the right angle in a right triangle.

33. The scaffolding used to erect walls consisted of *almojayas* (putlogs), the horizontal timbers encased in the rising walls, and *parales,* the vertical supports that stood parallel to the wall.

The *sardinel* is the support or threshold of the door in the habitation from jamb to jamb.[34]

The *talud* [footing] is an extension of the lower edge of a wall above the foundation level, the wall itself being less wide.

One should say *coluna* instead of *columna,* a term inappropriate to the profession.[35]

One should pronounce the term *petril* rather than *pretil* [balustrade or battlement], since it is the most appropriate pronunciation.[36]

Escantillon is the measure of a thing. It is a general term; thus *dar escantillon* means to establish the thickness of a stone, beam, etc.

A *danza de arcos,* or to draw a *danza de arcos,* is a succession of arches, whether on one or four sides.

Quebrantarse un techo [weakening of a ceiling] is a term used when a ceiling has too much weight on top of it, which depresses or warps it.

Terraplenar, narrowly defined, is to fill with earth, but the term is also used to mean fill up and compact a void, etc.

Calafatear [to caulk]. Caulking of fountains and house cracks is done with a chisel using resin spar and fine plaster.

The proper term is *cenefa* [border], not *zaneja,* as many improperly refer to it.[37]

A *faena* [task] is a labor requiring a short expenditure of time in some project, principally connected with festive days.

There are two qualities of adobe: one called *de marca,* the other *sancopinca.*[38] *De marca* is worth 6 reales per hundred, *sancopinca* 5 reales.

34. *Sardinel* also means brickwork in which the bricks are set on edge to form a molding such as an impost or a cornice.

35. *Coluna* was the accepted term for column in the eighteenth century; *columna* does not appear in the Royal Academy's 1726 dictionary. *Columna* is the preferred term today, however.

36. Both terms were used in the eighteenth century. Only *pretil* is used now.

37. *Cenefa* and *zanefa,* but not *zaneja,* were acceptable in the eighteenth century.

38. Both the guilds and the *cabildo* had an interest in regulating the quality of products to protect buyers from inferior goods. *De marca* means regulated in composition. *Sanc* means thick mud and *sancopincas* were probably bricks made without tempering material, such as straw, that prevented cracking. *Sancopinca* bricks doubtless came from the barrio of that name located in the northwest quadrant of Mexico City.

Ripio comes by the bag like sand, the price varying from one-half to two loads for 1½ reales.[39]

Salaries of Working Masons

The *oficial superior* [superior journeyman], 6 reales.
The *oficial bueno* [competent journeyman], 5 reales.
The *media cuchara* [person of mediocre abilities], 4 reales.
Peones [day laborers], 3 reales; or in many places 2½ reales.
Cabritos [youths who pick up debris], 1½ to 2 reales.
Soquiteros [men who mix mortar], 3 reales.

Payday is, by custom, on Saturday. Each laborer is paid for his work, withholding one real for meals given him during the week.

Nowadays the paver takes into account the number of bricks required in a room of so many varas in length and width. This should be known to the maestro.[40] Charges vary: it may be 2 reales per square vara or there might be instances where three-fourths real is charged for a square vara. For the 2 reales referred to they provide soil [in which to set the bricks] and the laborer, which are charged to the paver. For one, and even three-fourths, real the soil and laborer must be provided.

There are various maestros who work as painters. A blue border, the most popular, like other colors has different prices dependent upon the demand for a good design. There are those that may cost 4 reales per vara, and others of lesser intricacy that may cost one-half, three-fourths, 1, 2, or 3 reales. There are some borders that run

39. *Ripio* probably refers to crushed stone or brick used, like sand, as a tempering agent or grog in mortar. Vitruvius wrote that when river or sea sand was mixed with lime to make mortar, a third ingredient, pulverized and sifted burnt brick, should be added. See Vitruvius, *Ten Books,* 45.

40. Paving, whether of rooms or streets, was at this time as much within the domain of the architect as was designing a building. For example, the maestro mayor of Madrid, Jaime Marquet, was brought from France to supervise the paving of the streets of the capital. See George Kubler, *Arquitectura de los siglos XVII y XVIII.* Vol. 14 of *Ars Hispaniae* (Madrid: Editorial Plus-Ultra, 1957), 234–56.

twenty, thirty, forty, fifty, and up to sixty varas per peso. If a room is to be painted solely with red hematite, the entire room can be done for 1 peso or 4 reales, and the same prices prevail for marbleizing. If it is proposed to paint equestrians, etc., these may run from 6 to 10 reales apiece.[41]

Stonecutters work by the day or by the job. It is up to the maestro to determine whether the work merits 6 or 7 reales by the day; and if by the job, he has to pay according to the contract for the cut stones.

Pies derechos, A.[42]
Soclos, B.
Salmeres, T.
Bazas, Z.
Sobrebaza, X.
Those oriented to the inside *O, mochetas.*
Bazas at 5 reales, *pies derechos* at 1½ reales, *salmeres* one fourth more than one.

The facings *A* are called *paramentos* [facades]. A portal is composed

41. Painted dados were common in Mexican colonial structures, whose white-washed walls would quickly show staining and marring near the floor. The dado was usually painted a rust red, the source of the pigment being hematite, an iron oxide that was plentiful and cheap. Marbleizing was much in vogue in the nineteenth century.

42. This list apparently described the parts of a facade shown in one of the illustrations for the manuscript that are now missing. *Soclos*, in this context, probably are the lower parts of a wall that is distinguished from the upper wall by a different surface treatment and molding. The correct eighteenth-century usage designated the square plinth (now *plinto, zócalo,* or *sotabasa*) used under the pedestal or base of a column. However, the author applies it in a very loose sense. Another meaning of the term (*zoclo* in this case) is that of a course of mosaics or tiles placed at the foot of a wall of a house or room to prevent the wall from getting wet when the floor is washed. A *salmer* is a stone cut with one inclined edge and used as the first unit in an arch or vault springing from the impost. The author apparently had in mind any kind of voussoir. *Bazas* are pedestals or the bases of columns or pilasters above their plinths. However, in the description of a portal, the author appears to use the term to mean plinth. *Sobrebaza* is the author's own term. It appears to refer to the rounded elements (*bazas*) upon which a column or pilaster was seated. A *mocheta* is a cornerstone or quoin.

of a plinth of *tezontle* of one-fourth [vara], a cornice [to the pedestal] made of *chiluca* of one or two stones according to the desire of the hirer, a plinth and base [of a pilaster or column] of *chiluca*, [and] pilasters [or columns] of *cantería*, their number, according to the height of the door, from five to eleven stones.[43]

They commonly make plinths, bases, uprights, and lintels. From all these pieces they can make up a more ornate jamb with *moldados* [concave elements] and *acojinados* [carved elements],[44] moldings of half relief, and carved and concave elements of high relief.

There are doors with plinths, pedestals, bases, and uprights with bases made up of different panels and moldings as required by the composite order. These are used after finishing the architrave, frieze, cornice, stone triglyphs, and volutes. They differentiate these stones with the terms *esquinas* [outside corner angles], *rincones* [inside corner angles], *corridas* [courses, presumably the lineal stones of the frieze], and others with their various angles.

One should refer to *la linea* [boundary] rather than *la lignea*, which has a different meaning. One refers to the area of a surface to be measured. For example, a room of eight varas length and four varas width is said to have an area of thirty-two varas, which is understood as square varas.

Designing a door.[45] It is very essential to know how to design a door. To design a door one should be familiar with the following terms: begin without a scale, as in the example *A-B,* with leveling the foundation up to the footing where the door is drawn. *A-C* is the thickness needed for the wall. If we suppose that the door is two varas in height, one will make his divisions as illustrated:

The cornerstone, one-fourth vara.
The extrados, one-sixth vara.[46]

43. The author has failed to mention the pedestal, probably because it generally was made of *mampostería* (rubble construction) to save money, and he is writing here primarily about working with hewn stone.

44. The term *acojinado* comes from *cojin* (square cushion) and refers to a carving in that shape. It is synonymous with *almohadilla*.

45. This paragraph describes the parts of a door that apparently were depicted in one of the missing illustrations.

46. The author employs the word *trasdos* in his text, meaning extrados, the outer curved face of an arch or vault.

Width of the door, two varas.
The splay, the thickness of the wall.
Front of the pilaster.

Various Other Terms

Lechada [whitewash] is used for whitening. The finest is made entirely of stone or unslaked lime. To produce it, big pots are buried in the ground to provide a bulwark against explosion. Little by little, the stone is slaked with the necessary water, and afterwards the *lechada* is left to settle, the longer the better. The lime has to be selected as stated above.

Zulaque [pitch] is composed of lime, kids' hair, and lard that is pounded until it is the consistency of leather and later is made into slabs.[47]

Rodapié is a skirting added to reinforce a building weakened because its footing is of insufficient thickness. It is built against the foundation, its thickness dictated by the particular case.

Padrino de la pared [the wall's godfather] is the expression used for the plane of the wall that assures the same straightness apart from the moldings.

A low wall of rubble construction or cut stone built for some particular purpose is called a *cortina* [curtain]. As far as it continues in the same direction, it is so defined.

In architecture the cubic vara of a wall signifies the cost which is regulated for purposes of appraisals. To this end some are evaluated at 3 pesos and others at 20 reales.[48]

Cascajo is an old mortar which can be reused in small pieces for roofs when applied to a thickness of one-fourth to one-half vara.[49] There is another kind of *cascajo* used over earth in order to seal it so that anthills are not harbored in the terrace roofs.

47. *Zulaque* was used to seal pipe joints.

48. In writing about the appraisal of walls, Vitruvius made a distinction between walls of rubble construction and walls of brick. A rubble construction wall was expected to last only eighty years, so an appraisal deducted one eightieth of its original cost for each year it had been standing. A brick wall was evaluated at its original cost, provided it was still plumb. See Vitruvius, *Ten Books*, 53.

49. The current meaning of *cascajo* is gravel or debris.

Xalpaco is made from watery mortar, not *mescla terciada,* and serves as an undercoat to the whitewash.

Rules for Cubing a Wall

To evaluate a wall, let us suppose that Z has a height of 4 varas plus 1½ varas for the footing, a length of 5 varas, and a depth of ⅔ vara. Adding the footing to the height of 4 gives us a total height of 5½ from bottom to top. Multiplying the 5-vara length by the 5½-vara height produces 27½ varas. Multiplying the 27½ varas by the nominator of the fraction of the depth, which is 2, produces 55. Fifty-five divided by the denominator 3 leaves 18½ cubic varas. And by multiplying the result by the regulated price of either 3 pesos or 20 reales, as stated, one will have made his evaluation.

Principles for the Maestro

Never affect technical terms in front of the workers, because, not understanding them, they would only ridicule instead of praising them. Thus the general rule should be to teach them, using those expressions which they themselves use, telling them: "come here, son"; "pick up your little stick"; "that vara"; "nail it here"; "bring the ruler"; "put it here on top"; "take a walk around"; etc.[50] This is how one can maintain their respect.

Never forget what authors have written for us because no one knows better than they. According to the maestro, the critical obstacle to the profession is to master the elements of geometry, arithmetic, and stonecutting. One should apprentice himself to the most experienced architects. And even though those of the royal court may base their knowledge on mechanics, one should not mind them because, ultimately, they must surrender [to the superior knowledge of the authors]. In case the authors do not touch upon practical experience, everything taken into consideration is nevertheless unalterable, and when one is grounded in the general rules and accepted principles, he can cast aside those who would oppose what is right.

50. These commands are in the familiar rather than the formal mode. The practice has prevailed to the present time.

The Dominican monastery of Santo Domingo as it looked about 1850. The monastery, home of the Inquisition, had its own maestro mayor. (Manuel Ramírez Aparicio, *Los conventos suprimidos en Méjico*, Mexico City: J. M. Aguilar, 1861–62.)

Methods of Raising a Wall Without Causing the Collapse of the Second Story[51]

Let the walls be *A* and *B* with *B* resting upon *A*. The problem for the maestro is to raise wall *A* for some purpose without damaging the one to be built above. How do we accomplish this? Procedure: in the upper portion of the wall make some holes *L*,[52] and into them insert the joists *J* that rest on the ceiling *J* and its roof beams, which extend from *C* to *G*, and do the same on the opposite wall. Begin the extension at *M* so that at the same time the holes are being

51. In this very confusing description, the author apparently is giving directions for erecting a two-story structure, starting with the joists instead of the roof beams, that is, proceeding from top to bottom. This would probably be clearer had the illustration not been lost.

52. The holes to receive the joists are built up around the joists using stone and mortar, as the author explains in the ensuing sentences and paragraph.

made, roof beam *E-G* may be introduced, extending through the thickness of the wall *B* so it is seated comfortably and perfectly.[53] I declare now that even though the lower wall is raised, have no fear of the upper one falling.

Demonstration: the [joist] holes *L* formed of mortar and stone are of such strength as to appear to be a single element for the juncture of all its parts, like a vault. Later, if roof beams *J* are introduced and wall *A* is raised, wall *B* weighs upon this solid mass that is above the roof beams and roof. What can hinder this is that the parts *Z* have no support, and here the project could be jeopardized.[54] That is true, but since it is necessary to support it for only a short time while a crossbeam *E* is set in place which distributes the weight, there is no risk, and this has been proven.

To Proceed with Definitions

Air space of a house. This signifies no more than how much one is permitted to build in a vertical space. One buys this as well, so it follows that a house has two owners: one owns the ground and one owns the air. I think that there is an ordinance whereby houses can be no taller than a prescribed height, as one can believe from those constructed in this city.

A *mediania* is a common wall serving two houses. When construction is undertaken the two houses are joined in the middle, with both owners paying half the cost of the common wall. This should be noted in the deeds. Upon selling any air space, one should see if *medianias* are allowed, because that would increase the value as a saving to the buyer in building his house.[55]

53. Since the author is describing roof construction without the use of corbels, which help distribute the weight of the roof beams, he is saying that the roof beams must extend through the walls in which they are placed rather than be seated in the center of the walls.

54. "Parts Z" are the unsupported ends of the roof beams, or *vigas*, which rest on one wall while the other ends are being seated with stone and mortar in the opposite wall.

55. An example of the use of a *mediania* is what seventeenth-century documents referred to as a pair of houses, which meant two houses that shared a patio divided by a wall. Each house in such a pair was called a *casa sola*.

Alfardas are the inclined beams used to support a staircase which is not supported by a vault.[56] This type of staircase is called *de alfardas*.

Tezontle is called the divine material because of its grasping quality. Thus, even though the cut stones of a vault are not as perfectly cut as they should be, they are usable. This is not to say that vaults made in Mexico do not use cut stone, because one will see that the Indians make up for this imperfection by forming stones in the shape of long cones, cemented from above with rubble, *tezontle,* and strong mortar, so that from the top the bonding of all these materials makes it look like a porcupine. But one should be aware that they include cut stones.

Parts of an Ordinary Door

The principal parts of a door consist of three *cercos* [stiles], *peinazos* [upper rails], and *peinazones* [lower rails]. *Cercos* are the uprights to which the *peinazos* and *peinazones* are attached. The lower ones are also called *caneros.* The sill and lintel drilled with holes which enable the door to move is called the *chumacera* [pintle door]: the male member is the *quisialera,* the female member the socket. *De peinazo a peinazo* [from rail to rail] means the same as *de clavos a clavos* [from nail to nail] [and includes the] *medianias* [the panels between the rails].

Parts of a Beamed Floor[57]

Built directly on the ground is a foundation called a *soclo,* and upon this rest beams called *soleras* [plates]. Upon these stretch joists from one side of the footing to the other which help support the floorboards. What is illustrated for the middle applies to the sides *X-Z,* which are shown uncovered so that one might see the interior and the fact that the floorboards are borne above the footing.

56. *Alfardas,* in modern usage, are the supporting walls of a staircase, as well as the gradient support.
57. The illustration depicting the construction of a floor is missing.

Abuses of the Profession

1. To have to sign evaluations without having been paid. At times this is unavoidable, not having the money because the building has not been finished. There is no remedy for this.

2. They reject the *angel* who would become a guild member, an abuse born of the omission or ignorance of the maestros.[58] And since this is already established, it will not stop.

3. The royal engineer authorizes the memorandum of what the maestro mayor of the Royal Palace has earned in order that the viceroy may give him the draft of his earnings. And he may [or may not] order that they pay him since he holds little confidence in the maestro mayor.

4. That some architects may be making evaluations with no other qualification than their experience in finishing houses. This is not a rule, but a judgment which sometimes results in rash estimates, while, on the other hand, he may, under the allowances of this custom, be capable of knowing how to evaluate a vara of beamed ceiling, brick work, etc.

5. When a maestro accepts a job as a gift and does not visit it, the owner, or whoever is overseeing the work, is apt to make many errors. All the defects caused by others will be charged to the maestro, injuring his credibility.[59]

6. All maestros give themselves titles of mayores when this is reserved for the master of the Royal Works, a title granted, by luck, from the king. He should be the ultimate authority in the inspection of those [Royal Works] and all other things related to the profession. The rest [of the maestros] should sign themselves as "So-and-So, Maestro of this Noblest City" and "So-and-So, Maestro of the Works of the Holy Office, Convent, etc."[60]

58. *Angel* is an archaic term used to refer to a person with outstanding skill in some art or profession. Admittance into any guild appears to have been tightly controlled to avoid too much competition. Furthermore, sons of maestros took precedence over outsiders in being admitted to apprenticeship.

59. Actually, under terms of the new ordinances drawn up by the architects of Mexico City in 1736, the private individual was prohibited from building, either by himself or with only the aid of a foreman. See Toussaint, *Colonial Art*, 278.

60. A single architect might hold more than one title. For example, Pedro de Arrieta simultaneously held the titles "Maestro mayor del Santo Oficio" and "Maestro

Method and Technique of Making an Appraisal

"From So-and-So, maestro mayor of this Noblest City and of the profession of architecture in New Spain, named as an expert in the examination and evaluation of a house located on the edge of the Barrio de la Alameda, in behalf of the most reverend fathers of the Hospice of San Nicolás. I declare that, having inspected and measured the front that runs from east to west, I found it to be fifty varas and the side running north and south seventy-five standard Mexican varas. With respect to the neighborhood where the property is located, and according to the royal ordinance of this Noblest City, it is worth 250 pesos. At the same time there has been built on this property a structure of *mampostería* [rubble construction] in the modern style which is composed of a living room, bedroom, drawing room, kitchen, plus another room; all completely built with its corresponding roof and windows, and with iron [door] and window grills and railing. The rest of the site is taken up with eight rooms measuring seven square varas, each with two doors, one opening on the patio of the house, the other onto a small corral which serves each room. This house, as stated, is built of good *mampostería,* and having evaluated the materials, grills, windows, lumber, roofs, and other things along with the value of the site, I appraise the property at 5,935 pesos. Thus I declare and swear to God our lord and to the sign of the sacred cross that all may be legally known and understood and I sign it, etc.—So-and-So"

Maestro Mayor of the Royal Palace

1. Originally the maestro mayor was paid 600 pesos 200 reales for his work on the Royal Palace and 400 pesos for his work on the cathedral, but in the time of Señor Ahumada y Villalón, viceroy of this city,[61] a royal decree was promulgated whereby the *juez de obras*

mayor de este Reino y obra y fábrica material de la Santa Iglesia Catedral Metropolitana y de estas Casas Reales." See Francisco de la Maza, "El proyecto para la capilla de la Inquisición," *Anales del Instituto de Investigaciones Estéticas* 12 (1945): 19–26.

61. Agustín de Ahumada y Villalón, the Marqués de las Amarillas, became viceroy in November 1755. He held the position until his death on 5 February 1760, serving under Fernando VI and Carlos III. He was a reformer who attempted to control the self-aggrandizing officials of the previous administration, and he served

[justice of public works]—who is always an *oidor*[62] who serves without stipend—would suspend work on the Royal Palace and reduce the salary of the maestro mayor to only 200 pesos, while the payment of 400 pesos for the cathedral would be stopped. As a result of this, the canons have not been paying any portion [to the maestros], and this has come to be established policy.

2. To inspect the drainage ditch with the viceroys is politic but not an obligation, except for the maestro of the city.

3. According to a clause in his appointment as the maestro mayor to His Royal Majesty and of the works of the Royal Palace, he was paid 600 pesos annually with other emoluments that might pertain to the position. What is meant by emoluments are old locks, doors, escutcheons, wood, and old iron found in the works under his charge, but this was stopped by a viceroy.

4. The viceroy gives the order of payments by which the maestro mayor is paid his salary and his expenditures.

5. [It is considered] an impertinence for the maestro mayor to ask payment for a mere 20 pesos that he spent: an example is a whitewashing job that has required more than was estimated. Such small

---

with such disinterest that he left his widow without funds. She was able to return to Spain only out of the generosity of Archbishop Rubio y Salinas. Ahumada y Villalon is known for continuing work on the Royal Drainage Ditch. See Manuel Rivera Cambas, ed., *Los gobernantes de México* (1873; reprint, Mexico City: Joaquin Porrua, S.A., 1981), 1:379–85.

62. An *oidor* was a judge of the *audiencia*, a Spanish institution which represented a fusion of justice and political administration in the Spanish colonies. It was divided into two *salas* or branches: criminal and civil. In its juridical capacity it was the supreme tribunal, serving as the court of first instance for more serious crimes and as an appellate court for less serious cases. In its civil capacity the audiencia was a check on the powers of viceroys and governors, and it served those officials as a consulting body and assured the continuity of government when a viceroy, governor, or head of the audiencia died. The audiencia of the province of Mexico was established in 1528, and as the pacified portions of New Spain grew, new audiencias were added. The audiencia was composed of a *presidente, oidores* (who varied in number according to the particular audiencia), and lesser members such as scribes, notaries, and sheriffs. *Presidentes* and *oidores* were *letrados,* men trained in the law, and were collectively known as *justicias* (justices). The audiencia's involvement in building resulted from the *Recopilación,* or Law of the Indies, which stated that in cities where there was an audiencia in residence, any public work or building had to be done with the approval of the *presidente* or the senior *oidor,* and the *justicia* and *regimiento,* who evaluated the project's necessity, cost, and effects. See *Recopilación de leyes de los reynos de las Indias* (1681; reprint, Madrid: Ediciones Hispánica, 1973), Libro IV, Título 16, Ley 2.

sums are added up until there is a notable quantity [worth presenting].

6. This [example] is given in regards to viceroys and their wives who ask of the maestro small favors such as whitewashing a dressing room for them.

7. If the viceroy should die and the maestro has not collected, his money is lost because the royal officials do not pay without an order of payment.

8. Don Luís Navarro[63] lost 4,000 pesos simply because Señora Doña Ynes,[64] who came under royal patronage, lost the money through the death of [her husband] the viceroy.

9. The position of maestro mayor is now very oppressive, with only a 200-peso salary, and under the jurisdiction of the *oidor* or *juez de obras*, who may ask him to build his own structures and to visit them, and [request] a thousand other impertinences at no charge.

Maestro Mayor of the City

1. The maestro mayor of the city is elected by the *regidores* and deputies of the city.[65] His annual salary is 300 pesos with the obli-

63. Luis Díez (or Díaz) Navarro, born in Malaga, Spain, in 1699, worked on fortifications in Barcelona and Cádiz as a military engineer before coming to Mexico City in the early 1730s. He was employed on the fortifications of Vera Cruz and on the Royal Drainage Ditch before Viceroy Vizarrón on 9 February 1739 named him maestro mayor of the cathedral upon the death of the maestro mayor Pedro Arrieta. During his years in Mexico City, he also worked on the Casa de Moneda. He moved to Guatemala in 1742, and then in 1743 to Costa Rica, where he served as governor until 1750. Following his governorship, he returned to Guatemala, where he became one of the most important architects in Guatemala City during the second half of the eighteenth century. See Heinrich Berlin, "Artifices de la Catedral de México," *Anales del Instituto de Investigaciones Estéticas* 11 (1944): 35; and *Enciclopedia del arte en América* (Argentina: Bibliográfica Omeba, 1968).

64. Doña Ynez apparently was the widow of Viceroy Pedro de Castro Figueroa y Salazar, Duque de la Conquista y Marqués de Gracia Real. He was born in San Julián de Cela, Coruña, Spain. His term as viceroy, which began in August 1740, was cut short by his death in 1741 at San Juan de Ulúa, where he was directing the construction of new defensive structures. See Rivera Cambas, ed., *Los gobernantes*, 351–54.

65. A *regidor* was a councilman who served as a member of the *cabildo*, or municipal government. In the late colonial period the *cabildo* of Mexico City had fifteen *regidores* who held permanent, hereditary positions. They annually elected two *alcaldes*

gation of inspecting, with the *juez del desagüe,* the Royal Drainage Ditch of Huehuetoca at appropriate times, which are at the beginning of the rainy season or when there is some immediate danger to said project.[66]

2. He receives no emolument other than his salary, although when he changes doors or makes some repairs to the selling stalls of the plaza and secondhand stores, he is given 4 reales a visit.[67] And the owner of the stall gives him a pair of hose or other item of little value.

3. He has the responsibility of inspecting all the projects on city public lands without any recompense.

4. The *regidor de obras* is the one who actually runs everything and keeps up with materials. The maestro engages himself in nothing more than supervising his projects.[68]

---

ordinarios (magistrates) who possessed civil and criminal jurisdiction in courts of first instance. *Cabildos* held such municipal responsibilities as keeping the peace, overseeing sanitation, inspecting hospitals, maintaining public buildings and roads, regulating prices, and levying a militia.

66. Mexico City, which was built on an ancient lake bed, was surrounded by water and subject to flooding. The first attempt to control flooding was a dam constructed in 1449 under the king of Texcoco, Nezahualcóyotl. The dam, subsequently known as the *albarrada de los Indios* (Indians' Dam), was not effective and was damaged during the reconquest of 1521. In 1555 the Spaniards constructed their own dam, *albarrada de los Españoles,* and sought other ways to drain the water, but with unsatisfactory results. Determined to resolve the problem, the Marqués de Croix in 1767 began construction of the Royal Drainage Ditch of Huehuetoca (Real Desagüe de Huehuetoca, or Real Desagüe del Valle de México). Work progressed off and on through all the viceroyalties, but the project was not completed until 1895, under the administration of Porfirio Díaz. See *Diccionario Porrua: Historia, biografía y geografía de México* (Mexico City: Editorial Porrua, S.A., 1976).

67. Selling stalls were small wooden cubicles rented by the city to merchants and other businessmen.

68. The *regidor de obras* (*regidor* of public works) was a member of the *cabildo* who served as a clerk or majordomo of public buildings. In that capacity he was responsible for ordering and paying for building materials, hiring and firing workers, and paying salaries. The involvement of such administrators in the building trade was not without precedent. For example, numerous cases have been recorded for England, dating back to the Middle Ages. See Douglas Knoop and G. P. Jones, *The Medieval Mason: An Economic History of English Stone Building in the Later Middle Ages and Early Modern Times* (1933; reprint, New York: Barnes & Noble, Inc., 1967), 19–24, 30–32, 170–74.

5. In case of fire, he has the obligation of fighting it with Indian help using *barretas* and *cántaros*.[69]

6. He has the further obligation of collecting 9 or 10 pesos from each parish. In some areas such as San Andrés they pay in sugar. The entire amount goes to the *regidor de obras* to pay his office, unless the maestro secures or makes an agreement [to receive] that contract in which [the *regidor*] reaches an agreement for remuneration from the water works and thus becomes the sole contractor.

7. He has a thousand overseers such as the *corregidor*, the *regidor de obras*, and the superintendent.[70]

8. Any of these officials mentioned has the right to take him from his work to inspect any of the irrigation ditches, bridges, causeways, water conduits, commons, or other works maintained by the city.

Notices

In Madrid the maestro mayor draws a salary of 5,000 Mexican pesos, a house in the Royal Palace, a uniform, a baton [of authority], and [use of] a court *forlón*.[71] During 1755 the position was held by a youth who was only 23 years old.[72]

Sculpture, painting, and architecture are considered the three fine arts as conferred in Paris and all of Spain.

69. *Barretas* were iron bars used to break through doors and windows to get to fires. *Cántaros* were large clay jars used by water vendors. The responsibility of the maestro mayor of the city for fighting fires apparently dated from the Medieval period, when European guilds of builders were assigned, by municipal authorities, the task of fire fighting. See George Renard, *Guilds in the Middle Ages* (London: G. Bell and Sons, Ltd., 1919), 52.

70. A *corregidor* was a vice governor with both political and judicial authority who administered a given portion (*corregimiento*) of a province (*gobierno*) in the name of the governor. The *Recopilación* mandated that a superintendent and overseer of public works (*regidor de obras*) be appointed from among the *regidores*. See *Recopilación*, Libro IV, Título 16, Ley 3.

71. A *forlón* is a chaise with four seats.

72. The author probably was referring to Jaime Marquet, the French architect, who was brought to Madrid from Paris by the Duke of Alba to supervise the paving of the streets and who was favored by Fernando VI with such commissions as the plan for the city of Aranjuez, the palace theater, various other public and private buildings there, and the Casa de Correos in the capital. He died in 1782. See Kubler, *Arquitectura*, 14:219, 235, 259, 264, 267.

Water Conduits[73]

There is a map of the organization and reciprocal complex hidden underground. This is used for governing and policing the city and as [a guide] for selling water. Its layout is as follows: *A* is the reservoir and the others are branches by which [the water] is distributed. The water allocated for the city that enters through the conduits of Chapultepec is the best water and comes from Santa Fe. The other water source, which is heavier and less pleasing, is carried by the conduits of Belén and comes from the reservoir of Chapultepec. The hills of the latter are close by and serve as an upper reservoir so that the water is not dissipated. It is the work of the former Indian kings. Because of leakage from the reservoir it has been caulked.[74]

Advice Concerning Some Things

The architect should know that the rotting of the ends of pilings is caused by air and not water. Experience has shown that when they

73. There appears to have been an illustration, now lost, that showed the layout of the water system. The map of the underground system to which the author refers was drawn by Don Carlos de Sigüenza y Góngora. The author refers to it elsewhere in the manuscript. I could not locate a copy of the map.

74. Mexico City was supplied by two aqueducts. The first originated in Santa Fe, with springs from the Desierto de los Leones feeding into it as it flowed toward the city. This aqueduct, composed of 900 arches of *mampostería* and brick, was begun under the viceregal administration of the Marqués de Montes Claros (1603–1607) and finished under the Marqués de Guadalcázar, the viceroy in 1620. By 1710 its water, which was clear, was being distributed to 91 *mercedes*, or water grants, through branches serving the northern half of the city and its outlying barrios. By mid-century it supplied 7 public and 108 private fountains. In 1806 it supplied 27 public and 380 private fountains through a network of 6,135 varas (over 202,000 feet) of conduits that were divided into four branches. The *caja* (reservoir) of the Belén (also called the Salto del Agua) was fed by the springs of Chapultepec, which were stored in the *alberca chica* (an *alberca* is a reservoir of stone or plastered brick). Historians believe that the Belén aqueduct followed the same route as an aqueduct constructed by the Aztecs. The aqueduct, composed of 904 arches constructed of *mampostería*, was finished in 1779 during the administration of Viceroy Don Antonio María de Bucareli y Ursúa. Water from the Belén was referred to as *gorda* (fat) or *gruesa* (thick), for it was brackish and apt to be muddy during rains. By 1806 this aqueduct served 4 public and 125 private fountains through 4,924 varas (over 162,000 feet) of conduits that were divided into three branches. See Manuel Carrera Stampa, *Planos de la Ciudad de México*, Boletín de la Sociedad Mexicana de Geografía y Estadística, vol. 67, nos. 2–3 (Mexico City, 1949), 287–88.

have been found after many years in some foundations, those parts which were covered or buried are undamaged, while the distal ends which were uncovered and exposed to the air are rotted.

An example of how a journeyman might be fooled within the day: he may level and measure two varas of [mortared footing] in the morning and discover that it has shrunk three or four dedos, the material having been consumed and absorbed by the ground on which the wall rests.

I have heard it said that a church should be oriented in such a way that the principal door looks toward the west, to satisfy some rite of the church that I do not understand. When there are no other buildings to obstruct the site one should orient it as prescribed, but if buildings prohibit this, one builds where he can.[75]

Carved Work and Stone: Frontispieces

The frontispieces now popular are referred to as *obras de talla* [sculptured or carved work] and, truly, they have come to be nothing more than side altars on the street. The order in which the architect should proceed is the following. The design of the frontispiece should be made by an able painter, but this must be done under the directions given by the maestro to assure, for example, that the proportions correspond to the first and second registers, etc. Better yet, hire a master joiner to draw the plan, or, as others say, the front elevation.[76] Joiners are those artisans who make retables. It is said that they are familiar with designing front elevations and using moldings suitable to incorporating *boladas* [spherical elements] and *proyecturas* [other projecting elements]. The architect, before beginning the work, needs to examine and correct [the plan], because if he knows how to design, he envisages the plan which the joiner brings him. He will see if it is agreeable to the eye and if there are any defects to correct—for example, if it is not proportional to the

75. A preferred east-west orientation in sacred buildings with the altar at the eastern end predates Christianity. For example, Vitruvius prescribed it as long as there was no other structure blocking such an orientation. See Vitruvius, *Ten Books,* 116.

76. The joiner (*ensamblador*), a member of the Guild of Carpenters, was able to collaborate with the architect because he was also trained and examined in architecture *de lo blanco,* whereas the ordinary carpenter licensed *de lo prieto* was enjoined by guild ordinances from collaborating.

cornice or if the pedestals are not commensurable to the order they are designed for—because it is important that they properly support the Doric shafts, and other things of this tenor. Having corrected the design and having assured himself on all details, he will call in the stone sculptors and, with the overseer of the stonecutters, will confer on whatever is needed to begin the work. Thus they may work following the perspective and iconographic design without exceeding the limits set by the maestro.

Ingletes [diagonal angles of 45 degrees] are moldings that instead of being straight, break, forming a right angle, or 45-degree angle. It is made of the same molding as that used on the base [of a column].

Cepas is not a generic term, but only fits in some cases. For example, in order to make a foundation, a *cepa* is opened for its trench. To make an *escalera de bóveda* [staircase built over a vault] one opens *cepas* for its footing. To build a bridge one opens *cepas*. One does not use the expression "to open *cimientos* [foundations]," but "to open *cepas*."

The maestro should speak of *bolzores*, not *bolsones*.[77] This is a term of the stonecutter's art and can be found in illustrated treatises on the hewing of stone rather than in books of architecture.

The learned man knows what scaffolds are, but one should note that journeymen today realize as much from putting them up as they do in working in *mampostería*.

[They claim that] to test a cementing job, [one should] throw pitchers of water on the wall to see if it is absorbed or runs out the crevices of a bad job. This is a false [test], in my estimation.

A difficult problem for the maestro is to have a pilaster of one-and-two-thirds varas in height and two-thirds vara in width. He can construct it if he orders *pisietes* with custom dimensions of length, width, and breadth.[78]

One should note that the most learned masons should profit when the job expands. By the same token, he should profit as much

77. *Bolsón* is the equivalent of a *salmer*, the first stone laid in an arch.

78. *Pisietes* were normally cut in one-half vara lengths, slightly over one-third vara in width and one-fourth vara thick.

The monastery of San Francisco, which was one of the earliest to be constructed. Shown here is the Balvanera Chapel. Each convent and monastery had its own maestro on its payroll. (*Mexico y sus alrededores,* Mexico City: Decaén, 1855–64.)

as the [cost] of a project increases. Refer to Tosca at the end of his first volume of mathematics.[79]

Maestros of the Convents

Each convent of nuns pays its maestro annually: some pay him 100 [pesos] a year, others more, and others less. These maestros have charge of the houses, workshops, improvements, repairing the cells, and whatever else presents itself, such as on-site inspections, evaluations of materials, and examinations of nuns' cells. The maestro is

79. Tomás Vicente Tosca, born in Valencia, Spain, in 1651, was a mathematician, architect, and philosopher. His *Compendio matemático* was published in 1670. He was ordained a priest eight years later. His *Arquitectura civil* appeared in 1694 and his *Compendium philosophicum* in 1721. He died in 1723. For a summary of his architectural accomplishments in Valencia, see Llaguno y Amerola, *Noticias de los arquitectos,* 4:102.

paid by the majordomo of the convent. Although the maestro is not responsible for the bills for materials, he approves them for the majordomo. However, there are some convents in which the maestro is put in full charge of and handles the bills for mortar and materials, so that, in a word, all the money passes through his hands. But it is the norm for the majordomo to handle all this, with the maestro only affirming and examining the bills for what has been spent. Here is where the conscientious scruples of the maestro become important, because even though the majordomo might be very faithful to the evaluation of the overseer, he might, instead of recording four cartloads of mortar, put down five or six, and the poor maestro can never swear to the bills unless the expenditure passes through his hands. Doctor Don Manuel Rubio y Salinas wanted to find out how the income of the convents was being used.[80] He called upon the maestro mayor Don Miguel Espinosa de los Monteros, since that [knowledge] was outside the work of his [Rubio y Salinas's] jurisdiction.[81] Although the majordomos were anxious for him to affirm and swear to the bills, he refused [to countenence their expected] profit, giving as an excuse that he could not swear to what he had not seen; and that in order to swear to it, it was necessary [that they] stay within the [legitimate] limits and costs for materials.

Examination of the Architect

1. The examinee should appear before the supervisors of the profession in order that they may ascertain his suitability.[82]

80. Manuel Rubio y Salinas, appointed the archbishop of Mexico City, arrived in the capital in 1749 and died in 1765. During his tenure he erected numerous churches, fostered missions, and founded 197 parochial schools. See *Diccionario Porrua*.

81. Miguel Espinosa de los Monteros succeeded Luis Díez Navarro as maestro mayor of the cathedral on 3 September 1742. He was still holding the position in 1756. See Berlin, "Artifices de la Catedral," 36.

82. The examination required of the journeyman to obtain his *carta de examen*, or license, as maestro was ordinarily conducted by two *veedores* (overseers) who, as maestros, represented the guild; by a member of the *cabildo*, usually the secretary, who represented the municipal government that issued the license; and by two witnesses for the journeyman, who apparently insured that he receive a fair examination. See Manuel Carrera Stampa, *Los gremios mexicanos* (Mexico City: Ibero-Americana de Publicaciones, 1954), 38–39.

2. It is not necessary that the said examinee work as a foreman until he has gained sufficient practice and knowledge of the art. This is a juridically confirmed point, as witnessed by common practice born of certain lawsuits.

3. Neither are the ordinances to be followed the same as those treated by Father Lorenzo[83] in the book on architecture, but [those passed by] the patricians of the *cabildo*.[84]

4. The supervisors of the profession should designate a day for the examination that is convenient for the examinee. It may be held in any suitable house.

5. The examination consists of two parts: one morning and one afternoon, consecutively. The afternoon session covers studio work, the morning session actual labor.

6. The studio examination covers applied geometry, algebra, architecture, and stonecutting. These treatises one will find in the work of Father Tosca,[85] except for architecture that one can see in Uvolfio,[86] because he [Uvolfio] leaves nothing out.

7. The examination covering labor consists of constructing a pilater or a span of cornice or some other work, which he does with his own hands and which the secretary of the *cabildo* has to certify.

83. Fray Lorenzo de San Nicolás.

84. The guilds and *cabildos* maintained a complementary relationship in which the guilds policed their own membership and thus maintained standards which they themselves set, while the *cabildo* regulated trade and promulgated guild ordinances. The first ordinances governing the building trade were those of the Guild of Masons, passed by the *cabildo* of Mexico City on 27 May 1599 and confirmed by Viceroy Luis de Velasco I on 30 August 1599. They apparently were superseded by the ordinances of 1736, which were drawn up by a group of prominent architects in Mexico City and confirmed by the viceroy, the Archbishop Juan Antonio de Vizarrón y Eguiarreta. By those ordinances stonecutters and masons became subject to the Guild of Architects. For more information on guilds, see Carrera Stampa, *Los gremios;* and Francisco del Barrio Lorenzot, *Ordinanzas de gremios de la Nueva España* (Mexico City: Talleres Gráficos, 1920). An outline in English of the 1736 ordinances can be found in Toussaint, *Colonial Art*, 277–78. The original ordinances can be found in the Archivos del Antigua Ayuntamiento de Mexico, expediente no. 2983, legajo 14.

85. Tomás Vicente Tosca.

86. By Uvolfio the author probably meant John Woolfe, an Irish architect who, with designer James Gandon, wrote volumes 4 and 5 of the *Vitruvius Britannicus,* published in 1767 and 1771, respectively. The volumes are a survey of the architecture of the period, including Palladianism, which was very popular in England during the eighteenth century. Woolfe was an officer of Works, or the King's Works, an organization of top craftsmen who worked under royal patronage. Woolfe died in 1793.

8. A maestro also has to show the *cabildo* how to draw all kinds of arches or types of vaults on the wall. When this is finished, he presents himself to the *cabildo* to earn his *carta de examen* [license].[87] He will pay at that time a *media annata* [half a year's income] of 12 pesos 4 reales and other expenses of the office. Expenses for the title examination and the morning and afternoon examinations comes to 100 pesos, more or less.[88]

9. There are *de lo blanco* [white] and *de lo prieto* [black] examinations. The white examination covers the preparation of appraisals and working with buildings made of rubble construction and cut stone. The black examination is limited to the knowledge and practice of adobe construction and does not include making appraisals. One can say that it is an examination that can be conferred on any mason, even if he does not know how to read and write.[89]

10. The maestro can find evaluations in the *audiencia* office where many evaluations are made for purposes of auction.[90]

11. There is much work involved with the evaluations of *capellanías,* but this task has its particular maestro.[91]

87. The *carta de examen* (license) included the maestro's name, age, birthplace, and physical description. It gave him legal permission to pursue his trade, to have his own shop with apprentices and journeymen, and to enjoy the privileges of the profession, and it admonished him to uphold the ordinances. It was signed by the examiners, with the date, location, and the maestro's mark recorded in the margin. The maestro, when establishing a new residence, presented his *carta de examen* to his new town's *cabildo* for approval, much like the medieval mason who proved his mark when moving to a new lodge. See Carrera Stampa, *Los gremios,* 41.

88. The *media annata* differed considerably from place to place, even within the same guild. A *media annata* of 12 pesos 4 reales was high compared to 5 pesos 4 reales 6 granos, which was the more usual examination fee throughout the eighteenth century in Mexico City. A fee of 100 pesos for overall expenses must have been difficult for the average journeyman to pay. See Carrera Stampa, *Los gremios,* 209–10.

89. Historians have known that the *de lo blanco* classification was employed in the Guild of Carpenters, but this manual is the first document making the distinction between *de lo blanco* and *de lo prieto* in the Guild of Masons and Architects.

90. Private lands were sold at public auctions by the audiencia to satisfy debts or to pay defaulted taxes. According to the *Recopilación,* each audiencia maintained a book containing evaluations of the residences in its district in order to advise viceroys and presidents of the audiencia on the interests (*premios*) to be charged, perhaps in case loans were made against them. *Recopilación,* Libro II, Título 15, Ley 165.

91. A *capellanía* was a house donated to the audiencia with the stipulation that the rent from it would go toward a particular purpose, such as paying for masses for the dead or paying for the education of an impoverished youth who wished to enter the clergy.

Part of the examination to obtain the master's license required the journey-man to demonstrate his knowledge of all kinds of arches and vaults. (Denis Diderot, *Dictionaire des Sciences,* Lucques: V. Giuntini, 1758)

12. There are few appraisals in the Real Audiencia because experience shows how little there is to do.

13. Finally, no appraisal is acceptable unless signed by a licensed maestro. This is a good practice because the *alcaldes mayores*,[92] through the king's security bonds, regularly put up his properties as collateral against tributes. Bills and contracts substantiate the appraisal of the maestro so that the king may know the value of a building, and this is the reason why the evaluation has to be done by a maestro.

Instruments and Books
Which the Maestro Should Have

He should begin with the mathematical compendium of Father Tosca.[93] He should study the Euclidean principles in the same order in which they are set forth. He may afterward want to pursue other treatises, including that on military architecture, since it sheds much light on the practice of civil architecture and stonecutting.

Item. A set of Serrano's *Universal Astronomy*, which, although not concerned with architecture, covers an expanded treatise on geometry that is essential to the architect to comprehend its applicability.[94]

Item. A set of Father Laurencio's[95] writings on architecture, which, in comparison to Father Tosca's shorter treatise, are not as good, but nevertheless shed much light on understanding it [Tosca's] and present other information, above all in teaching the terms and material language of the maestros.

Item. A [volume of] Uvolfio, because what he wrote on archi-

92. *Alcalde mayor* was another name for a vice governor or *corregidor*.
93. Tomás Vicente Tosca.
94. Gonzalo Antonio Serrano was a Spanish physician, mathematician, and astronomer from Córdoba who published several works during the first half of the eighteenth century: *Teatro suprenio de Minerva, con su católico decreto y sentencia difinitiva a favor de la phísica, astrología, etc.* (1727); *Apología pacífica medicopráctica y rayos luminosos de Apolo* (1739); and *Tablas filipicas, católicos o generales de los movimientos celestes* (1744). His *Astronomía universal theórica y práctica, conforme a la doctrina de los antiguos y modernos astronomos* was published in 1755. See *Bibliographie générale de l'astronomie*, vol. 1, part 2 (1889; reprint, London: The Holland Press, 1964).
95. Fray Lorenzo de San Nicolás.

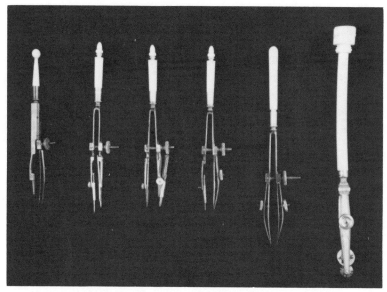

A set of ivory-handled eighteenth-century drawing instruments such as a new maestro might own. (Courtesy of Maria del Carmen Olvera C.)

tecture is so special that one should not want any other subject matter. He wrote on the mixture of mortars and other skills not to be found in any other author.[96]

To my way of thinking, these authors are more than enough for any maestro. The instruments which the maestro should have are the following: to draw plans and not have the points of the compass dig into the paper, one should have a firm, well-made drafting table, perfectly smooth, and if this could be made of bronze, so much the better. It should be at least one-half vara in length and width.

Item. An *estuche* [*de dibujo*][97] and all its instruments and the use of a pantometer such as seen in Father Tosca.

Item. A large, well-made level of wood with a plumb, all carefully made.

Item. The following maps: the map of water works written and

96. John Woolfe.
97. An *estuche de dibujo* was a drafting set containing compasses, angle rule, rulers, and other instruments.

published by Don Carlos de Sigüenza needed to discharge one's duty in overseeing all the circuits around this city.[98]

Item. A price guide. It is not a perspective map but only an ichnographic plan used to make appraisals.[99]

Item. A perspective map of the city. This is only a curiosity, but it serves as an adornment for the studio. At the top is the image of Our Lady of Guadalupe with the [coat of] arms of Mexico. This map accompanies the other.

Item. The map of the water conduits mentioned above, by which one can see where water grants are located and comprehend the workings of the conduits with their spouts and other things corresponding to the water works.

There are the principal maps. There are others of various hamlets, villages, and cities, for example, the printed work of Villaseñor, which treats [the history of New Spain] up to the discovery of California.[100] Even though it is very thick, it is enlightening to the understanding of the kingdom.

Item. A protractor for floors which serves as a sundial. One should know how to design the four vertical clocks because they are placed on the terraces of colleges and private houses.[101] One should be able to design them if he has seen the ninth volume of Father Tosca's treatise on geometry.

Item. Drawing paper and parchment on which to draw buildings, and here I would offer the following advice to the maestro:

1. That the elements of the ground plan be painted in colors.

98. Don Carlos de Sigüenza y Gongora (1645–1700) was a Mexican-born poet and cosmographer who taught mathematics at the Universidad Real y Pontífica in Mexico City. Appointed by King Carlos II as royal cosmographer in 1680, he authored the *Libro astronómica y filisófica*. See *Diccionario enciclopédico hispano-americano* (London: C. H. Simonds Company, n.d.).

99. The author used the word iconographic but obviously meant ichnographic.

100. José Antonio Villaseñor y Sánchez, a geographer and mathematician, was responsible for numerous publications on Mexico during the eighteenth century. His *Descripción general de los reinos y provincias de la Nueva España* (1746) probably included the map referred to here. See *Diccionario enciclopédico Espasa* (Madrid: Espasa-Calpé, S.A., 1978).

101. The making of clocks had been within the province of builders since ancient times. "There are three departments of architecture," wrote the Roman builder Vitruvius, "the art of building, the making of timepieces, and the construction of machinery." See Vitruvius, *Ten Books*, 16.

2. That stair landings be distinguished from steps on a plan, as in the illustration where they are denoted as *A, B,* and *C.* On the aerial view of the stair, one should note the number of treads seen in *B, E,* and *F.* The distances between parallel treads are called *huellas.*[102] See above where the formation of a stair is treated.

3. The ground plan should be indicated with parallel lines of the same dimension as the wall thickness to show the spacing of doors, from cornerstone to extrados and splay, and each part of the plan should be identified by function: storeroom, coach house, accessory.

The maestro should have a carpenter's square and *cordeles* to level and square whatever he is working on.[103] And given the consonance of this profession with that of surveying, he should have his water level with its stand, a cabinet clock with pendulum and bell, plus a reliable *muestra* for field work.[104]

Item. A good protractor with triangles for calibration with the geometric scale. All this should have a portable table with three legs and a directional compass. He should have *cordeles* marked in varas according to the standard of the city. It seems to me that this list is sufficient to carry out one's work unless he should want to look into and pursue purely mathematical matters, in which case he would need other instruments.

Catalog of Public Works in This City
Pertaining to the [Duties] of the Maestros

1. Works of the Royal Drainage Ditch of Huehuetoca.
2. Works of the aqueduct of Chapultepec.
3. Works of the Royal Palace.[105]

102. The illustration of a staircase is missing. In recent usage, *huellas* are synonymous with *peldaños* or *escalones,* while risers are known as *peraltes* (treads) or *contrahuellas.*

103. *Cordeles* were hemp cords used for surveying land or measuring buildings.

104. A *muestra* was a clock without a bell.

105. The viceroy's original Royal Palace was the Casas Viejas de Moctezuma, which was the house of the conqueror Hernan Cortés, located on the plaza west of the cathedral. The Casas Nuevas de Moctezuma, owned by the descendants of Cortés, was purchased by the crown in 1562 and modified to serve as the viceregal palace.

4. Works of the sacred church and sanctuary.[106]
5. Works of the estate and Marquesado del Valle.[107]
6. Works of this most noble city.
7. Works of the Holy Office.[108]
8. Water works.
9. Cleaning of the city and its irrigation system.
10. Inspection of surrounding public inns, commons, and bridges.
11. Inspection of streams and watersheds.
12. Works of the convents.
13. On-site inspections and appraisals of properties to be sold at public auction as ordered by the tribunals.
14. Either general or particular appraisals.
15. Specific works.

Opinions Which the Maestros Should Present

When there is some point of difficulty on a project concerning completed or planned construction, the maestro conducts an on-site inspection. It is important that he detail what he presents, but here is the general method in which the maestro should respond. This response he may call a judgment or an opinion of the maestro. An explanation of the methodical order and progress of his work is included. If it is work needed on a paved road [or causeway], he will calculate what it will cost. If it is [a problem connected with] the

106. The first cathedral in Mexico City was constructed between 1524 and 1532, reconstructed in 1585, and razed in 1626. It was replaced by the present structure, which was begun in 1573 on a new site but was not completed until the early nineteenth century. The last architects engaged in its completion were José Damián Ortíz de Castro (from 1787 to 1791) and Manuel Tolsá, who succeeded Ortíz de Castro. See Toussaint, *Colonial Art*, 109–10, 409–12.

107. The Casas Viejas de Moctezuma, the first residence of Cortés, who was the Marqués del Valle.

108. A flurry of building activity by the Inquisition occurred in the seventeenth century to accommodate the imprisonment of numerous wealthy Portuguese and the confiscation of their property. The harassment of the Portuguese, under charges of judaizing, appears to have been carried out after Portugal regained her independence from Spain. Inquisition properties in Mexico City included the palace, or residence of the inquisitors, the Holy Tribunal, a chapel, jails, and appendages such as kitchens. See de la Maza, "El proyecto para la capilla," 19–26.

water conduit, after having it leveled, he will look at the areas through which the water flows and will state, for example, that a certain part, because of the porosity of the soil, requires a stone and mortar conduit and that over such a distance it will be carried over twenty or more arches, and that from here to that part it can continue in an open ditch with the rest. He should take great care in his estimate of spaces so that later he is not held accountable [for a discrepancy]. At the same time he will give the measurements he has taken and present his arguments on what should, or should not, be done, all in considerable detail. If some church is about to fall or has fallen into ruin, he will present [his plans] for restoration and work that is appropriate so it will not collapse. He should resort to the laws of statics, watching for any part of the building that settles. Then he should offer his evidence, saying that if a certain portion bears too much weight it will fall, or that the skirting should not be in this place but in that other, and he should produce his evidence with [level] lines to satisfy the parties. If he offers opinions on an aqueduct or subterranean conduits, he should provide the necessary measurements to the majordomo or administrator of the *haciendas de campo* so that he may order [replacements] made of clay.[109] What I mean to say is that he should give the diameter of the conduits, together with the thickness, so that [in cross section] they appear as two concentric circles (as shown in this figure). The [administrator] is in charge of the replacement, but the maestro should provide the measurement. If it pertains to an *alcantarilla*,[110] he [the maestro] should see how many *interesados* [holders of water grants] are involved and determine who bears the cost.[111] At the same time, he should verify the *mercedes* [water grants] of each in order to give the measurements of the pipes in the present figure. As an example, the plan of the aqueduct of La Santísima Trinidad has four grantees.

109. There were two types of *haciendas,* one for livestock (*hacienda de ganadería*) and one for agriculture (*hacienda de campo*).

110. The use of the term *alcantarilla* to mean aqueduct is archaic. It currently is used to mean a small bridge, culvert, drain, underground sewer, or, in Mexico, a public fountain.

111. The term used by the author for holders of water grants is *interesados.* The requirement that they share the cost of repairs apparently derived from an extension of a law whereby the construction and repair of bridges and roads was paid for by those who benefited. (*Recopilación,* Libro IV, Título 16, Ley 1). The illustration which accompanied this section is missing.

Thus, as one sees, the sides of the aqueduct have holes *A, B, C,* and *D* which are the pipes that descend to the ground to divide [the water]. *A* is the grant of the Pila Real, *B* that of the Baño de la Santísima [Trinidad], *C* the Baño de Santa Teresa, and *D* the Pila de San Lázaro y Santa Cruz.

In Making Appraisals the Maestro Should Observe the Following Procedure

1. He should be accompanied by an Indian mason to measure the front and depth of the building to be evaluated, and he may want to take another companion to write up the appraisal with his notes.

2. He should carry a notebook and pencil.

3. He should draw front and side walls, note their orientation to east and west, or north and south, since it is advantageous that the four winds [directions] be included in any appraisal.

4. Enter the names of the contiguous buildings, or their owners, small plazas, and other landmarks of the neighborhood.

5. Make a brief sketch of ground and aerial views of the building.

6. See if there is a *mediania* which would add to or subtract from the bill as stated above.

7. Inspect the floor and ceiling beams, puncturing them to determine the presence of dry rot. Partitions and load-bearing walls should be hit with some solid object to determine whether they are adobe.[112]

8. Finally, recognize additions and include all appendages in the résumé. Calculate ironwork by pounds, arrobas, or *quintales* and how much it is worked. A brickwork ceiling can be evaluated from the number of square varas and its condition.[113] Include whatever else has value and, having determined the value of the cubic vara in the neighborhood, the appraisal will be made.

112. Partitions (*tabiques*) might be made of adobe or brick as well as wood. Hence the two tests relating to their soundness.

113. The term for ceiling brickwork used in the text is *enladrillado,* which ordinarily refers to a brickwork floor or pavement. In this case it refers to thin bricks which were laid across beams as a ceiling, sometimes in a herringbone pattern. Roofing tiles were used at least as early as Roman times. See Vitruvius, *Ten Books,* 57.

Extract of Various Sites with Their Evaluations
For Quick Reference The Maestro Should Consult the Map.

Portal of the Mercaderas: 80 reales.

Houses belonging to the state: 74 reales.

Street of Santo Domingo: first [block], 48 reales; second, 58
reales; third, where it ends at La Cruz de Tabarteros, 64 reales.

Royal Customs House: 48 reales. Corner of the Inquisition
and its street: 24 reales.

Street of the false door of Santo Domingo: 20 reales.

Bridge of Santo Domingo: 18 reales. Descending the bridge:
18 reales.

Portal of Santo Domingo: 32 reales. Small plaza of the monastery: 18 reales.

Street to the west of Santa Catarina: 8 reales.

Corner of Santa Catarina: 8 reales. Turning to the south: 12
reales.

Lane that goes to Santa Catarina: 6 reales. In its ultimate distance: 8 reales.

Square before Santa Catarina the Martyr: 6 reales.

Small plaza of Santa Catarina: 8 reales.

Señora Santa Anna: 1 ½ reales.

Bridge to the south leading to the city: 4 reales.

Square that comes before the bridge of Santo Domingo: 12
reales.

Turning to the west behind Santo Domingo: 12 reales.

The irrigation ditch behind the Misericordia: 8 reales.

Street behind San Lorenzo: 8 reales.

Street of San Francisco to the corner of Echavárri and the turn:
80 reales.

Front of San Francisco: 32 reales.

Following block and its corner: 35 reales.

The other [corner] where it terminates: 46 reales.

That [block] before La Professa: 56 reales.

Front of La Professa: 56 reales.

Following block: 64 reales.

Corner of Las Brigidas and bridge of San Francisco: 24 reales.

Front of Las Brigidas: 16 reales.

Corner in front of Santa Isabel: 30 reales.

Portals of Las Tlapelerías: 80 reales. Its facade: 80 reales.

Corner of the street of La Palma: 58 reales.

Street of Espíritu Santo: 42 reales.

Portico up to the old coliseum: 42 reales.

[Portico] to the new coliseum: 36 reales.

Street of the new coliseum: 36 reales.

Colegio de Niñas [girl's school]: 24 reales. Its corner in front
   of the fountain: 32 reales.

From there toward the east: 48 reales.

Corner of El Angel: 48 reales.

Street of Las Capuchinas: 48 reales.

From there to the corner where the Hogal Press is located: 52
   reales.

Street of La Monterilla: 72 reales.

Street of San Bernardo: 54 reales.

Small plaza of El Bolador: 72 reales.

Royal University: 48 reales.

Street which continues to PortaCoeli: 40 reales.

Grills of Balvanera: 40 reales.

Bridge of the Correo Mayor: 40 reales.

Street of the barracks: 40 reales.

Street of La Merced: 40 reales. To its corner: 32 reales.

Front of La Merced: 24 reales.

Corner of the bridge to there: 20 reales.

Descending the bridge: 6 reales.

Bridge of Manzanares: 4 reales.

From there to Alamedita: 2 reales.

San Lazaro: one-half real.

From here to the west. Bridge of Pacheco and the fountain: 1
   real.

Descending the bridge: 2 reales.

Street which follows in the same direction: 4 reales.

San Juan de Dios: 8 reales.

Santa Vera Cruz: 12 reales.

Water reservoir. Bridge of La Mariscala: 16 reales.

The first block of San Andrés: 18 reales.

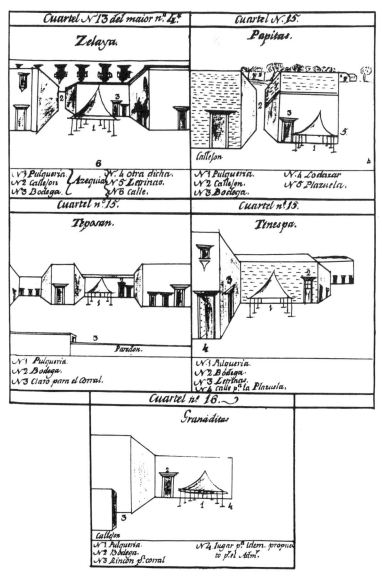

Pulque shops (*pulquerías*), which were controlled by the government, were probably built and owned by the city and leased to proprietors. This plan for pulque stalls for the military barracks of Mexico City was drawn in 1794 by Ignacio de Castera, then maestro mayor of Mexico City. (Courtesy of the Archivo General de la Nación.)

Second block in front of Los Betlemitas: [no evaluation].

The first block of Santa Clara: 32 reales. Second block: the
same.

Street of Tacuba: 40 reales.

Corner of the same: 56 reales.

Front of the Alcaicería [raw silk exchange] to the east, where
[there] are houses belonging to the state, [and the] corner
of Tacuba: 74 reales.[114]

Street of the *acequia* [irrigation ditch]: 40 reales.

Street of Jesús María: 32 reales.

Bridge of the Leña: 20 reales.

Descending the bridge to the east: 6 reales.

Street of the Pulquería de Pacheco (I mean Pulquería de Palacio): 4 reales.[115]

To Santa Cruz: 2 reales.

Buildings of this barrio: one-half to 1 real.

Puesto in Monserrate: 8 reales.[116]

Behind San Gerónimo to the north: 8 reales.

Following street: 8 reales.

To that of Alfaro: 22 reales.

Corner of San Agustín: 24 reales.

Following street: 32 reales.

Corner of El Angel: 48 reales.

Street to the bridge of Espíritu Santo: between 48 and 50
reales.

Street of Espíritu Santo: 55 reales.

Street of La Profesa to the south: 40 reales.

That which follows: between 28 and 40 reales.

That which follows to the south: between 28 and 18 reales.

That which follows: 16 reales. To the side of Santo Domingo,
which they call Pila Seca: 12 reales.

114. The houses belonging to the state were the Casas Viejas de Moctezuma,
or Palace of Cortés.

115. According to the *Recopilación*, the number of *pulquerías*, or shops where
pulque was sold, was not to exceed thirty-six in Mexico City: twenty-four for men,
twelve for women. (*Recopilación*, Libro VI, Título 1, Ley 37.)

116. *Puestos* were public stalls leased by the city to small merchants and businessmen.

A *puesto* in the Salto del Agua for La Concepción to the north: [no evaluation].

Salto del Agua: 6 reales.

Following block: 12 reales. And the same for the street of San Juan to the right to the hospital: 2 reales.

Santa Isabel: 30 reales.

Reservoir: 18 reales.

La Concepción: 8 reales.

Front of La Concepión to the east: 2 reales.

Barrio of San Juan de Dios, San Hipólito, and Santa Vera Cruz: 2 and 4 reales, depending upon the boundaries, so that the main ones are 4 reales, the inner ones 2 reales, and the *abarrada* [dam] to the north one-half real.

Puesto near Regina to San Lorenzo: [no evaluation].

Small plaza and fountain: 10 reales.

Bridge of the street of Los Mesones [the inns]: 16 reales.

Following street: 22 reales.

That which follows: 24 reales to the Colegio de Niñas and 36 reales to the street of the new coliseum.

That which follows: 32 reales.

The other to the north as we have seen: 24 reales.

The following: 8 reales.

To San Lorenzo: 8 reales.

Puesto in the parish of San Sebastián to the false door of Santo Domingo: [no evaluation].

In this barrio: one-half real.

Following block and the turn toward El Carmen: 4 reales.

That which follows to the east: 6 reales.

The other to the false gate: 6 reales.

Puesto in San Sebastián to the back of San Gregório from there to the east: 4 reales.

Corner of this street: 6 reales.

Following street: 7 reales.

The street which follows, up to the east bridge of Santo Domingo: 8 reales.

Inner side of the dam facing Mochas: one-half real.

Inner side of the dam facing Monserrate: one-half real.

To the bank of water: up to 3 reales.

San Antonio Abad, San Antonio Tepito: one-half real.

Workshop of San Pablo and sawmill: one-half real.

Dam of the *acequia* and Pipis: one-half real.[117]

What follows is the edge of the *acequia* to the Puente de Curtidores which follows to the north, from 1 real, up to La Merced with its value of 20 reales.

The pulque shop of Santo Thomás and from here to the bridge of Santiaguito: 3 reales for said pulque shop, to one-half real [for the remainder].

Dam of La Palma and kiln: one-half real.

Dam of Santa Cruz: one-half real.

That [dam] of San Lazaro: one-half real.

That [dam] of San Sebastián: one-half real. The more remote part: to one-fourth real.

Santa Cruz Acatlán: one-half real.

Barrio of Santa Ana: one-half real.

Barrio of Santiago with its proportionate share of water: one-half real.

Barrio of Santa María: one-half real.

Behind the Casa de Conchas: one-half real.

Following block behind La Santísima Trinidad: 12 reales.

Corner in the same direction: 12 reales.

Up to the Hospicio [Amor de Dios]: 16 reales.

Street of the Hospicio: 28 reales.

Corner of the Hospicio: 26 reales.

Old street of Santa Teresa: 30 reales.

Solano bridge: 4 reales.

Following block: 6 reales.

The one which follows up to Jesús María: 8 reales.

Printing press of Jesús María: 14 reales.

Closed street of Del Parque: 20 reales.

Turn to the north: 32 reales.

Street of Santa Inés to the east: 24 reales.

117. A Puente del Pipis is shown on maps dated 1853 and 1896. See Jorge González Angulo and Yolanda Terán Trillo, *Planos de la Ciudad de México, 1785, 1853 y 1896* (Mexico City: Instituto Nacional de Antropología e Historia, Departamento de Investigaciones Históricas, 1976), 17, 73.

Street of El Amor de Dios: 24 reales.

Lane of the same to the east: 18 reales.

Block which follows up to La Santísima Trinidad: 14 reales.

Block of the Colegio [de Santos] and false door [of Merced]: 8 reales.

Following block: 4 reales.

That of Pacheco: 2 reales. And up to the bridge: 1 real.

Small plaza beyond: one-half real.

Being in San Juan de la Penitencia, its small plaza to the north: 5 reales.

That which follows to the west: 4 reales.

Continuing in this direction: 2 reales.

A block to the west: 1 real.

Trees and dam to the west: one-half real.

Standing in the center of San Juan with its lanes to the south, the first: 3 reales.

The second: 2 reales.

The third: 1 real.

The fourth, the Plazuela de los Caños to the north: one-half real.

Little plaza to the east of the center of San Juan: 6 reales.

Street of San Juan to the east: 12 reales.

Second block to the east: 16 reales.

Street of San Phelipe Neri: 22 reales.

Its corner: 24 reales.

Corner of the street of the Arco [de San Agustín]: 24 reales.

Street of the Arco [de San Agustín]: 24 reales.

Exit from the street of Jesús to the north: 48 reales.

Street of Jesús to the east: 32 reales.

Small plaza of Jesús to the east: 32 reales. To the north: 48 reales.

Street of the Parque del Conde to the east: 16 reales.

Block of Jesús to the east: 12 reales.

Street of Posadas: 10 reales.

Block following, its first corner: 8 reales.

The other [corner]: 6 reales.

The bridge: 6 reales.

Descending this bridge in the same direction: 3 reales.

Plazuela de la Palma: 2 reales.

Dam: one-half to three-fourths real.

As it continues: one-half real.

Opposite Las Mochas: one-half real.

Belén de Mercenarios: 2 reales.

A block to the east: 3 reales.

Salto del Agua: 4 reales.

Farther toward the east: 8 reales.

Calle Real which faces directly the Colegio de San Pablo: [no evaluation].

Small plaza of the Salto del Agua: 8 reales.

Calle Real which follows: 8 reales.

That which follows to the east: 8 reales.

Street of Monserrate: 8 reales.

Monserrate and behind San Gerónimo: 8 reales.

Street behind San Miguel: 8 reales.

Block which continues to the fountain of San Pablo and its corner: 8 reales.

Small plaza: 6 reales.

Following block: 4 reales.

Up to the bridge: 4 reales.

Bank of the *acequia* which follows: 2 reales.

Dam: one-half real.

Small plaza of El Carmen to the west: 4 reales.

Corner of the state house: 74 reales.[118]

Turn of the street of Tacuba: 64 reales.

Escalerillas: 64 reales.

Street of El Relox: [no evaluation].

Calle de los Cordovanes: 40 reales.

Puesto in the waterfall as it goes toward [Niño Perdido] Piedad and Calzada: [no evaluation].

First block: 6 reales.

The last block before the bridge and sentry box: 2 reales.

Puesto in San Fernando: one-fourth real.

San Hipólito as it follows: 1 real.

Block up to San Juan de Dios: 4 reales.

Block where the Casa de Concha is located: 2 reales.

118. The Casas Viejas, also known as the Marquesado, Palace of Cortés.

That which fronts San Diego: 3 reales.

That which fronts the Alameda: 4 reales.

Corpus Christi: 5 reales.

Barrio of La Santa Vera Cruz, San Juan de Dios, San Hipólito, and San Fernando from those closer in toward the northwest: one-half real; one-fourth farther out.

Enclosure around the Ejido de Concha y Horca: one-fourth real.

Behind Corpus Christi: 2 reales.

The dam from here to the southwest: one-half real. The more distant [portion]: one-fourth real.

Puente de los Gallos, or the corner to behind La Concepción to the south: 8 reales.

As it continues to the east behind San Andrés: 13 reales. To where it completes the block: 18 reales.

Following block to the east: from 24 to 28 reales.

That which follows: from 32 to 40 reales.

From here to the corner of Santa Teresa: up to 12 reales.

The total frontage of San Camilo: 12 reales.

San Joseph de Gracia: from 12 to 20 reales.

Stalls which were returned to the portico of Santo Domingo from La Encarnación: 26 reales. That which follows which pertains to Bergara: from 32 to 24 reales.

One will note that many streets are missing from this extract and that those that are listed are treated with brevity. Yet one is advised that the maestro will have recourse to the map in addition to the prices, which will vary at the same time.

Land surrounding the city is regulated as pasture land.

Since 5,000 pesos is the maximum value allowed for a *caballería* of irrigated land, a vara of land is thus worth less than one eighth.[119]

Civil architecture is a science which teaches one how to design and build with strength, proper proportions, and beauty. Although its professors are regularly referred to as *arquitectos*, *alarifes*, and maestros mayores, in the strictest and most rigorous [sense] they

---

119. A *caballería* was a piece of land 100 feet wide and 200 feet long. (*Recopilación*, Libro IV, Título 12, Ley 1.)

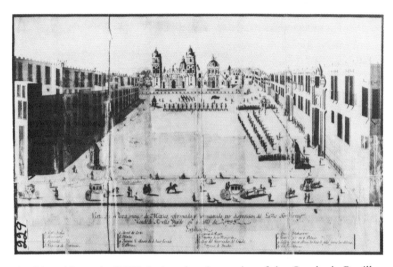

The Plaza Mayor in 1793 during the viceroyalty of the Conde de Revilla-gigedo, about the time when this manual was written. (Courtesy of the Archivo General de la Nación.)

should be called arquitectos and maestros mayores of "whatever," depending on the work with which they are charged, such as the city, the Royal Palace, or the Holy Office.

Following the rigorous sense of the law, the architect is the chief of all structures or constructions, calling himself the leader because he is the principal builder responsible for the plans of the arches, vaults, etc. It is not necessary that he be a mason as some would like him to be. It is enough that he be proficient in architecture, drawing, and stonecutting, and that he be able to design any sort of arch or vault. This is the point now authorized by the Real Audiencia.

In this royal Mexican court there are two types of maestros: one, recognized as the principal one, in charge of His Majesty's Royal Works, and a second in charge of the works of our most noble city. The first is in charge of the works belonging to the king. His salary used to be 600 pesos: 400 pesos for work on the cathedral and the remaining 200 for the Royal Palace. The position was maintained with this salary up to the time of Count Revillagigedo, when His Majesty ordered suspension of the revenue for [construction] of the cathedral, leaving the 200 pesos.[120] This is the total compensation for this position, even though his title suggests that he enjoys the salary along with the rest of the emoluments pertaining to it. It should not be understood that he is able to realize the price of old woodwork, ironwork, etc., that he might plunder from the Royal Palace, but [must depend] solely on the referred-to salary. Accordingly, the position is today very impoverished.[121]

120. Juan Vicente Güemes Pacheco de Padilla, the Conde de Revillagigedo, was born in Havana in 1740 and served at Gibraltar as a lieutenant colonel. He was named viceroy by Carlos III and arrived in Mexico in October 1789. He was considered one of the finest men to serve in the position and was responsible for pushing through the progressive policies and Bourbon reforms of Carlos III. He died in Madrid in 1799. See Rivera Cambas, ed., *Los gobernantes,* 1:472–87. The reduced building activity of the second half of the eighteenth century was probably linked to the precarious state of Spain's economy. Spanish involvement in the American Revolution was considerable, and the empire loaned to the American colonists 1½ million–pounds' worth of silver mined and minted in Mexico. Mexico furthermore bore the expense of defending the Philippines from the British, who wanted the islands. The unavailability of mercury for amalgamating the silver, due to interrupted shipping, caused a drastic drop in silver production, with a consequent spiraling inflation rate and increasing tax demands after 1779. The result was a drastic reduction in all domestic programs. Toussaint suggests that another reason for the reduced attention to the cathedral in the eighteenth century was that the interior was finished enough to be used for services. Building was resumed, however, toward the end of the century, when Ortíz de Castro built the towers of the cathedral, beginning in 1787 and finishing in 1791. And a new cupola was designed and built by Tolsá at the end of the century. See Manuel Toussaint, *La Catedral de México* (Mexico City: Editorial Porrua, S.A., 1973), 64, 67.

121. The author's claim that the jurisdiction of the maestro mayor in charge of the king's Royal Works had been reduced in the 1790s to just the maintenance of the palace, with a consequent reduction in salary, supports Heinrich Berlin's contention that in the 1700s the position of maestro mayor had become largely honorific, while architects without the grandiose title actually planned and executed major projects. For example, in the same period that the maestro mayor in charge of the palace was making only 200 pesos a year, the architect Ortíz de Castro was being paid 1,000 pesos per year for his work on the towers of the cathedral, and he did not have the title of maestro mayor. That dubious honor was held by Francisco Guerrero y Torres, who was largely ignored. Berlin also notes that ecclesiastical authorities, the *cabildo ecclesiástico,* replaced civil authorities as administrators of cathedral construction. That perhaps accounts for the absence of documents in the Archivo General de la Nación pertaining to the building after 1723. See Toussaint, *La Catedral,* 64–67; and Berlin, "Artifices de la Catedral," 36–38. The restriction of the maestro mayor of the Royal Works to work on the Royal Palace in the 1790s also explains the appearance in late colonial documents of separate titles of maestro mayor of the palace and maestro mayor of the cathedral.

A major hardship is that it is difficult to profit from this position. The maestros mayores who practiced some fifty years ago here might collect interest on the buying of materials because of owners who wanted them to lower by half or a quarter [the price] of wood, lime, etc. This is still a just solution because the engineer has always had his palm greased in this city for being in charge of the materials and signing the bills so His Excellency might authorize the order of payment and he [the engineer] might be paid from the Royal Treasury.[122]

Considering What a Foundation Is Able to Bear

Should the maestro be called upon for a structure and he is aware that old foundations might be used to save labor, time, and material, he should certify that the foundation is still sound.

Preparation: the test might be like those in branches of mathematics. He might figure a cubic vara of that same rubblework wall, verify the air weight on a Roman scale, and then make his calculation in this manner. Operation: he calculates the mass of all the walls and the roofs with their brickwork, beams, etc. He will add up all the cubic varas and multiply by the hundredweight of a cubic vara. He will thus derive the hundredweight that those foundations bore.

At the same time the maestro, working from the plans he has drawn, can calculate the cubic varas, and should they exceed those of the former, he will declare that those foundations are not suitable. However, should they not exceed [those of the former] he will declare that the foundations are usable in the same state in which they remain.

Given a *pisiete* whose height is two thirds, breadth one fourth, and thickness one sixth, figure how many *pisietes* are needed for a pilaster of a cubic vara. For example, this problem is the Achilles' heel of maestros. It can be resolved in this manner and is the general rule [to be followed] for similar problems [in calculating] mass.

122. The expression *la mano lebantada* in the manuscript is a rendering of *venir con sus manos lavadas* (to come with clean hands), used to describe someone who expected to realize something without having labored to earn it.

Operation: to determine the mass of the *pisiete,* calculate the mass of the pilaster which is the whole, divide by the mass of the *pisiete,* and one knows how many there are.

Example: arrange the *pisiete* to calculate it in this manner. To cube it, multiply the width by the length, and that by the breadth. It will be the multiplication and mass of the *pisiete.*

This is to say that if we divide the cubic vara into seventy-two parts, one part constitutes a *pisiete.* Let us go on to the second step. Divide one into seventy-two. We still have a complete form because the value of the whole is seventy-two. In this case there is nothing more to say but that there are seventy-two *pisietes* in this same pilaster.

Note that as one cubed the *pisiete* one can cube the pilaster when one determines the dimensions, for example, given twelve varas height, four varas width, and two varas breadth, one goes through the same operation.

Finally, the divider, like the dividend, should be of the same denomination.

Terms for the Designing and Cutting of Stone[123]

1. Each worked stone consists of six surfaces.

2. *Y-M* is the *dovela interior* [double interior]; *F-G-H* is the *dovela exterior* [double exterior].

3. Surface *F-M* is the *paramento* [facing] and *cara anterior* [obverse facing]. Its opposite *F-H* is the *paramento* [facing] and *cara*

123. The author extracted items 1 through 7 in this section from Tosca's *Tratados de arquitectura civil,* which defined the stonecutter's art. Tosca's explanation used different spellings than did this author, who by changing the spelling of key words obscured Tosca's definitions. Tosca's explanation reads: "Las piedras de que se componen los arcos y bóvedas, imitan la forma de una cuña, como se ve in la fig. 1. Constan de seis superficies, de las quales la interior *I-M* es cóncava, y se llama dovela interior; su opuesta *F-G-H* es convexa, y se llama dovela exterior. La superficie *F-M,* que suele ser vertical, se llama paramento y cara anterior; y su opuesto *I-H,* paramento y cara interior. Las otras dos superficies *F-I,* se llaman lechos o juntas, por juntarse y servir de lechos las de unas piedras para las otras. La superficie sobre quien asienta y ajusta otra, se suele especialmente llamar lecho; y la que asienta sobre el sobrelecho. La piedra que esta en medio de un arco o bóveda, se llama clave; y las primeras a uno y otro pie, incumbas o bolsones." (Tomás Vicente Tosca, *Tratados de arquitectura civil, montea y canteria y reloxes* [Valencia: La Oficina de los Hermanos de Orga, 1694].)

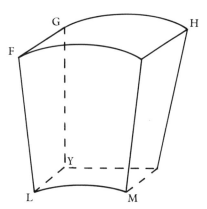

The facets of a keystone, which the author derived from Tomás Vicente Tosca's *Tratados de arquitectura civil.*

interior [inner facing]. The other two surfaces, *F-Y* and *H-M,* are called *luchas* [*lechos*] or *juntas* [joints]. The other surface upon which another rests and fits should be especially referred to as the *lecho.* And the one above it is the *sobre lecho.* The stone in the middle of an arch or vault is called the keystone. The first stones laid on either side of an arch or vault are *incumbas* or *bohares* [*bolsones*].[124]

4. *Cimbria* or *cerchon* is the plank, or planks, cut with the same curvature as the arch.[125]

5. The gnomon or carpenter's square is a well-known instrument consisting of two rulers forming a right angle.

6. A *saltaregla* is another well-known instrument composed of two movable rulers connected at a point in the mode of a compass [and] with which any angle can be measured and transferred to the stones.[126]

7. *Regla cercha* or *baivel, escoda* [stonecutter's hammer], *cincel* [chisel] or *tallantes* [chisel?].[127]

8. When all the junctures or courses of an arch or vault con-

124. *Bolsones* or *salmeres,* the first stones laid in an arch or vault, are the terms used today.

125. In the eighteenth century, *cimbria* was used interchangeably with *cimbra* to designate the wooden support used when constructing an arch. Only *cimbra* is used today.

126. The author followed Tosca in using the term *saltarella* even though the 1726 Royal Academy dictionary used *salta regla.* The hinged ruler was a cross between a compass and a ruler with a semicircular device for reading angles.

127. In the eighteenth century a *regla cercha* or *baivel* was a stonecutter's instrument forming a *mixtilíneo* angle equal to that of the foundation stones or *salmeres* of an arch. A *mixtilíneo* is a Spanish arch form employing both straight and curved lines.

verge toward a point, one says that the stones orient their *tirantes* toward that point.[128]

9. When the first stone on one or the other side of an arch is level with the horizontal plane, one uses the expression *mover de quadrado* [to spring from a squared stone].

10. When [the stone of an arch] is seated on an inclined plane, one uses the expression *mover de salmer* [to spring from a *salmer*].[129]

The Santuus Santa Santorum, according to the Hebrews, was the most secret part of the temple where no one but the high priest entered.

Engineer: *leg. si putater ad leg. aquilig.*[130] He is the one who makes machines, but according to Ulpiano,[131] *leg. ult. d. simens fatig.*, etc. The measurer says that the difference [between the engineer] and the surveyor is that [the former] measures fields with a perch of ten feet.

We Shall Speak of Examinations And of the profession [of architecture], its teachers, and ordinances to be observed.

The number of maestros in this court has never exceeded eight nor been under four, which is cause for admiration when we see the surfeit of individuals in other professions. I declare that eight is a sufficient number to take care of all the works. It is a profession

---

Modern dictionaries identify a *cercha* as a wooden rule for measuring convex or concave objects, while a *baivel* is a square bevel used by stonemasons. *Tallantes* are unidentified.

128. *Tirante* is now used to indicate a joist or tie-beam. The author apparently used *tirantes* to refer to the mortared lines of an arch which converge to the vanishing point.

129. The author lifted the definitions of *mover el arco de quadrado u horizontal* and *mover de salmer* directly from the Royal Academy's 1726 dictionary. The first expression might apply to a flat arch in which a lintel is replaced by voussoirs and a keystone, a polygonal arch such as the Spanish *ochavado*, or a stilted arch (Spanish *peraltado*) in which the spring line is raised by vertical piers above the level of the impost. The second expression, *mover de salmer*, refers to any of the circular arch forms which begin with a *salmer*, the first voussoir with the top surface inclined toward the horizontal plane of the bottom surface.

130. The Latin in this paragraph cannot be translated.

131. By Ulpiano the author means Dometius Ulpianus, Latin jurist and prefect of the Praetorium, who served under the Roman emperors Septimius Severus, Caracalla, Elagabalus, and Severius Alexander until his assassination by the praetorians in

requiring common knowledge, and thus we see some teachers, even though they may have inherited the art from their fathers, unemployed because they do not know [the profession].[132] It is not like other professions in which, upon obtaining their licenses, they proceed on the credit of their predecessors.

It is [a profession] like the rest of the liberal arts, but in this country it is controlled by the guild. During Holy Week [members] assume the role of angels and are furthermore obliged to march as a unit when some war makes it necessary.[133] For this reason a captain and other officers are designated in conformance with the militial ordinance issued by the captain general, His Excellency the viceroy. I do not recollect having read that they [accordingly] enjoy certain privileges as one sees in other professions.

In the court at Madrid, a French youth who was not yet 23 years old held the position of maestro mayor with a salary of 8,000 pesos. He had a uniform, baton, home in the Royal Palace, and a coach from His Majesty's household [at his disposal].[134] In light of this, the maestro mayor [of Mexico] ought to petition His Excellency to raise his salary.

General Terms Used by the Maestro in Giving a Legal Description of a Site

1. A maestro is well paid who has to contradict unsettled [testimony] through a well-presented declaration in competition with

---

228. His judgments were so sound that they survived as one-third part of the Justinian Code. See Will Durant, *Caesar and Christ,* vol. 3 of *The Story of Civilization* (New York: Simon and Schuster, 1944), 634.

132. Sons generally followed their fathers' trades. The sons of maestros had precedence over others in being admitted as apprentices.

133. Guilds were social as well as economic organizations, and each had its *cofradía,* a mutual aid society that not only brought a religious unity to the guild under a patron saint, but also fostered a sense of community and cooperation. Members participated in both religious and secular functions, aided poor or sick members, and buried their dead. All guild members were required to march in the Holy Week processions, in which each guild was identified by its distinctive colors, standards, symbols, and the artifact from the Passion which it carried (architects and masons originally bore the crown of thorns). The patron of the Guild of Masons (later the Guild of Masons and Architects) was Nuestra Señora de los Gozos (Our Lady of Delights). See Carrera Stampa, *Los gremios,* 79–127; and Toussaint, *Colonial Art,* 278.

134. Jaime Marquet.

other maestros. Since the latter do not know the points of law, they are not able to articulate like the juridical architect, who can persuade and present faultless reason on some point on which he is qualified to speak. Here is a résumé of everything one could want to know on the subject.[135]

2. The term "of the edifice" derives from *quasi edium factio et est edium constructio*. However it can also be applied to *pro omni structura* [the entire, or every, structure]. In the definition according to Ulpiano,[136] *leg. si fund. qui fundis de legatis l.* [it is read in the first law that if one builds on foundations]—not only the area is intended, but also the ground on which the edifice has been constructed. *Edificare est eq. facere secu construere* [to build is the same as to make something or to construct] is understood as *pro reficere* [to rebuild], that is, to remake or rebuild. *Leg. 20 de mortis inferendis* [in the twentieth book of law covering bringing in the sick], a self-contained edifice *est idem atq. continum secu continuatis* [it is the same as contiguous or joined together]. *Leg. 17 de aq. pluv. ancend. et leg. Urbis appell. de Vento. significat* [in the seventeenth book of laws covering rainwater and the book of the city, called "Concerning Wind," it signifies that] because the building might contain under itself; *edis dimune,* which is the house *casamentiz forum havitatienz tabernas.* In this manner [his declaration] gives the architect reason for his own signification in each case.

3. The term *lotes* [plots of land] that has not been used there consists of two parts, according to jurists. It combines the meaning of ground and area. *Leg. solumid de rervend.* This is understood as area in everything built on the ground.

Prospective maestros should be examined in due form before the secretary of the *cabildo,* who is the one who authorizes the title or *carta de examen.* The two *veedores* [overseers] elected for that year should ascertain his aptitude in the study of geometry and its application, as well as its speculative aspect, and of arithmetic. This examination does not require that applicants have been laborers or stonemasons. This point has been determined by one Don Diego Dávila, auditor of the cathedral, who brought the lawsuit against the

135. Only some of these Latin phrases can be translated. The spelling of recognizable Latin words has been corrected from the original text.

136. Dometius Ulpianus.

veedores of his time. Although he wanted to be examined, the *veedores* would not allow it. And the Real Audiencia, under the acting prosecutor, thus entered into the law decrees that they [*veedores*] might examine them [candidates] solely on their proficiency in geometry.[137] But this does not stop the *veedores* from giving examinations covering public work, and from demanding that [the candidate] build a pilaster or a length of cornice according to his own plan. This demand should not be viewed as demeaning since even kings have set cornerstones of temples, using trowels of silver or gold which they have had made [especially] for that purpose.

The expenses of the examination are 100 pesos, which is enough for refreshments and the expenses of the judges. A half-year's salary is not above 8 pesos, which is comparable to other professions of mechanics. If they are examined *quod,* or as they say, *de lo blanco,* they have the faculty of understanding all sorts of appraisals by which they can be called upon by ecclesiastical and secular tribunals. But if they are examined *de lo prieto,* that is, examined without knowing how to read and write, they should only undertake adobe houses without calculating the cost, and no one may do it for them.[138]

The duties of the maestro mayor have been enumerated, but in relation to that office it appears advisable to me to give notice [to the maestro] that there is a *juez de obras* [building inspector] to serve in the position of overseer. In the event that some tasks have been [faultily] performed for the maestro mayor, he should not assume the full responsibility, but pay for the materials used and protect himself against such incidents, since there is a *juez de obras* who oversees the project.

In relation to the maestro of the city, who is also maestro of the Royal Drainage Ditch, he alone has the duty of on-site inspection of the latter, not the engineer or the maestro mayor [of the Royal Palace], except in the case of imminent flooding. He collects his salary from the work of the Royal Drainage Ditch. I said that the exception was the imminent danger of inundation because in this case

137. This law must have superseded the ordinance of 1736, which specified that each applicant for the maestro's examination must have worked six years as a journeyman. The text here indicates that guild officials defied the law.

138. The meaning is that the mason, examined *de lo prieto,* could build the house, but the plan and evaluation had to be drawn up by a maestro who had been licensed *de lo blanco.*

The church and hospital of San Hipólito, which at one time had as its maestro José Damián Ortiz de Castro, who designed the commemorative monument at the corner of the atrium. Ortiz also was engaged in work on the cathedral from 1786 to 1791. (Manuel Ramírez Aparicio, *Los conventos suprimidos en Méjico,* Mexico City: J. M. Aguilar, 1861–62.)

all the connoisseurs of the profession are obliged to level, to sound, and to keep track of the pending water and to do whatever is needed with assistance from the *oidores* and decree from His Excellency to impede [the waters] or to raze any building or rural property, etc., even though it may be church property.

In regards to the political control of this position, a warning is given to the engineer and the maestro mayor that their excellencies do not authorize payment of small bills, anticipating one of notable quantity to be paid. An example might be a small sum submitted for small repairs such as whitewashing a room. It would be considered an impertinence for the maestro to request authorization for such a small thing.

Buildings of Special Note

A hospital must have a fountain and infirmaries located near the nurses and chaplains. Street entrances are needed for the chaplain's and nurses' quarters, but not to the infirmaries, pantry, kitchen, *atolería*, etc.[139]

A palace (it is said that no building should exceed its height), as part of its peculiar structure, has jails and dungeons with windows through which the sun reaches the poor imprisoned people, fountains, water closets, privy houses or latrines, and, in view of all, a chapel or oratory on an eminent elevation, thick walls which double the usual, with the same for the foundations, bakeries, necessary offices, and quarters in the mode of workers' barracks.

Shops where pigs are sold have shown through experience that pig lice penetrate the walls.

Convents with Water Grants[140]
A cruciform church should be four times longer
than its width.

One without a cruciform should be at least the same.

If, with the crossing, the body of the church is two-and-a-half squares, it follows that the drum with its cupola must be one [square] and the presbytery constitute one square by which, in this case, the entire church would have four-and-a-half squares.

With five squares there would be three up to the crossing, one for the drum, and the other for the presbytery. This is the best, given in round numbers.

We now come to the crossing. This should measure half the width of the nave on each side.

The same can be said of the chapels: that they should be half the width of the nave in depth.

Should the church consist of three naves, each of the two sides should be half the width of the center aisle.[141]

In the four dimensions of the expressed measurements the thickness of the walls should be included. See the following figure:

139. An *atolería* was the place where *atole* was made or kept for the sick. *Atole* was parched maize flour ground and mixed with water and sugar or seasonings to make a drink or gruel.

140. The manuscript includes no text under this subheading.

141. In this somewhat confusing section, the author appears to suggest a ratio of 1 to 4 for church dimensions, based upon the square and its fractions. To what

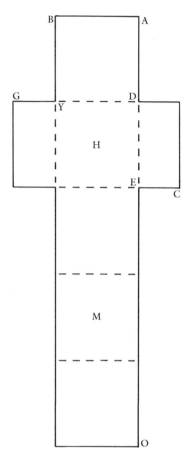

The plan of a cruciform church, based on the author's description.

extent this formula was followed is not known. The dimensions of fourteen varas width by fifty-six varas length provided by the architect Ignacio de Castera for the Oratorio in Querétaro, built between 1786 and 1802, is in the ratio of 1 to 4, with half squares ascribed to the sanctuary, choir, and arms of the cruciform. The Capilla de la Inquisición, designed by Diego de los Santos y Avila in 1659, called for the ratio of 1 to 3.6. See "Una carta del arquitecto Ignacio de Castera," *Anales del Instituto de Investigaciones Estéticas* 10 (1943): 82–83; and de la Maza, "Proyecto para la Capilla," 19–26. According to analyses I have made of colonial churches in Baja California and Texas, the lengths are best explained by square root extensions from a basic square that is generally derived from the maximum width of the structure across either the transepts or the towers. The lengths I have measured vary from the square root of five to the square root of eight.

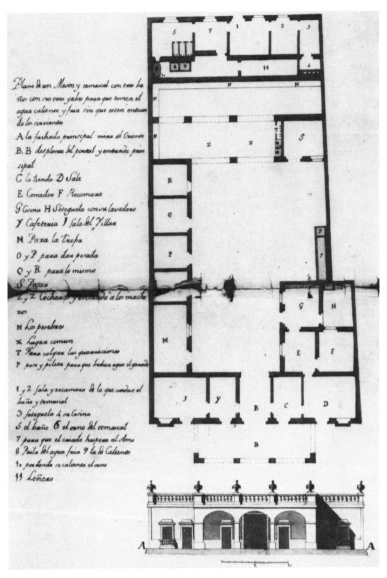

Plan and elevation for the Casa Mesón in Tacubaya, drawn in 1810 by Mariano Falcón. The drawing is typical of those described by the author. (Courtesy of the Archivo General de la Nación.)

O-B is the width determined by the architect.

The line *O-A* accounts for five widths which forms the parallel as *A-B*. The church has the figure of three squares up to *H*. *M* is the body of the church, followed by the crossing, which forms a square *Y-E* and the presbytery *D-B*. The crossing is another square *C-G*, everything emanating from the square *C-D*, which is half of *O-B* on each side.

The architect should prepare three plans or descriptions of any edifice: ichnographic, orthographic, and scenographic. The ichnographic description delineates the plan of the edifice. The orthographic one describes the profile and the scenographic shows it in perspective.

Bricks should neither be left unfired nor overly fired. If they are overly fired they become vitreous, and if they are left unfired they are not resistant to bad weather and melt to nothing in a short time.

Tepes or *céspedes* are blocks of sod mixed with grass roots. Straw is added to the adobe to increase its bonding. This type of adobe is not used for [load-bearing] walls.

Bedrooms should be square. Service rooms should be elongated to the extent of the square's diagonal.[142] Anterooms and receiving rooms should have *sesquatierra* proportions, that is, the width is two thirds of the length.[143] Drawing rooms should be in the ratio of

142. The appropriate dimensions of rooms were handed down from ancient times. Vitruvius wrote that atria should be designed with the ratios of 3 to 5, 2 to 3, or the square root of 2, while dining rooms should be 1 to 2. These ratios reflected increments of the square: a 3-to-5 ratio represented 1⅔ squares; a 2-to-3 ratio represented 1½ squares. The square root of 2 was obtained by giving the room the length of the square's diagonal. Ceiling heights were proportionately derived. Those of oblong rooms were one half the sum of the length and the width. Those of square rooms were one and one half the width. See Vitruvius, *Ten Books,* 177–79. Palladio followed Vitruvius's proportions, for the most part. He wrote that rooms might be round, square, or rectangular with lengths representing 1⅓, 1½, 1⅔, or 2 squares or the square root of 2. The 1⅓ rectangle (ratio of 3 to 4) is the only one not mentioned by Vitruvius. Palladio argued for the same ceiling height of oblong rooms, as did the Roman builder, but indicated this as the height of the vault. He differed in wall heights for square rooms. If those rooms had flat ceilings, the wall heights should equal the width; if vaulted they should be one-third part higher. (Andrea Palladio, *The Four Books of Architecture* [1738; reprint, New York: Dover Publications, Inc., 1965], 27.)

143. The author probably meant *sesquitercio* but misunderstood the proper

seven to four and ballrooms or banquet rooms should be twice as long as wide. All [rooms] should be a bit higher than their square.

Calerías are the kilns or ovens where lime is made.

A cistern is the receptacle where water is stored.

Theater. *Aherando impicundo* is a Greek word signifying a place to stage a play.

Amphitheater is a theater, but in its strictest sense it is a place formed by two theaters.

Quarries. The jurist calls them *latemias. Sucurrio ex causis.* The place where stones are cut.

Alberca [reservoir]—*piscina* or place where water is collected and stored.

One should say *chafranado* and not *achaflanado.*[144]

One should say *derramos* and not *derrames.*[145]

Excavar [to excavate] is the same as *cavar* [to excavate, form a cavity] or *sacar tierra* [to remove earth].

Aeromantic calculations are used in measuring the mass of walls, etc.[146]

Brocal is the curbstone of a fountain or well.

---

usage of the word. According to the Royal Academy's dictionary, in eighteenth-century Spanish the prefix *sesqui* meant a whole quantity plus the number added to it. For example, a square with the addition of one third was referred to as a *proporción sesquitercia*. The Spanish usage thus varied from the contemporary English meaning of adding one half to a number.

144. *Achaflanar* means to chamfer or bevel (*achaflanado* means beveled). In the eighteenth century the word was written *chaflanar. Chafranar* may have been a colloquialism, for it is not found in the Royal Academy's dictionary.

145. In this case the author is correct. *Derrames* is not included in the Royal Academy's dictionary. Apparently the colloquial term prevailed, and both terms are appropriate today to describe the splayed openings of doors and windows that permit the doors and shutters to be opened obliquely so that more light can enter.

146. What the author meant by this expression is impossible to ascertain, for aeromancy was divination from the state of the air.

Architectura mechanica conforme la practica de esta Ciudad de México

Protesta que hace el Autor

En los Libros de Architectura como se verá por el contexto de este escripto y sus parraphos, que aunque se tocan algunos puntos de geometria es solo de paso en quanto se enseña el Methodo de aplicarlos ala practica, y esto es mui distinto de como se tratan las Materias en los Libros. Enseña cosas nuevas del Arte que hasta ahora no (quizá) se habran escripto, lo que se a echo afuerza de mucho travajo, y de andar Collectando noticias, assi por lo que toca a Sitios, y precios (que su maior validacion certeza y corriente, ocurrirra el Maestro al Mapa, y Constumbre que el tiempo ofrezca; como se dice en su lugar). Del Goviermente Politico, del Arte; y sus terminos corruptos como se versan en las Bocas de los operarios, sin dejar de quando en quando de introducir algunos puntos Juridicos, como tan importantes para que el Maestro pueda dar una legitima Declaracion en qualesquier Juzgado.

En todo me sugeto ala Correccion Cristiana ala enmienda y Enseñanza de qualquiera de mifacultad (aunque no aya alarde de ella por su humildad, o no necesidad vale).

Todo lo que aqui se trata no esta
en los Libros de Mathematicas Terminos,
Govierno y Practica

Suelos.   Lo primero para una fabrica es el Suelo; su valor se
regula en varas quadradas; y cada vara tiene su precio segun el parage
en que se halla, por el Mapa de los precios, que se hizo reformando
el antiguo, en una junta de cavildo en tiempo de el Señor Rexidor
Don Antonio Davalos.

Maestros mayores.   De esta facultad se titulan mayores, respec-
tivamente de la obra publica que tienen asu cargo. Verbi gratia don
Fulano de tal, Maestro de los Reales Fabricas: De el Estado, Santo
Oficio etc. En la Ciudad hay un Maestro mayor, de que se tratará
despues, con todo lo añexo, asus quatro quadrantes, carretones, cañerias, y obra de el Real Desague de Huehuetoca. El Maestro mayor
del Real Palacio tiene su sueldo annual por Su Magestad y tiene asu
cargo las obras pertenecientes al Rey.

Cimientos, o Zanjas.   No metemos aqui los de los Templos porque en esto es fuerza arreglarse alos Authores. Hablamos pues de
casas regulares con sus altos, y entresuelos. Alos cimientos regulares
se les hecha una vara de ancho; y de profundo vara y media, o dos
varas fuera de el estacamento.

Alturas i gruesos de Paredes.   Segun el precitado cimiento,
desde el Taluz hasta el enrraze del primer techo tres quartas de
grueso, desde este asta el alto, dos tercias, o media vara. Las Aces-
sorias, o Zaguanes cinco varas de alto, los entresuelos tres varas, y el
alto de arriva seis, sino se echan entresuelos, seis y media varas abajo,
y seis arriva: todo esto es aduitrario.

Tabiques.   Los de abajo media vara, los de arriba una tercia, esto
es lo regular, pero segun Aleman podrán adelgasarse hasta una
quarta.

Estacamento.   Despues de señalado el cimiento con una poca de
cal en polvo, se abre el cimiento para señalarlo, se saca aplano, y recto
con la Esquadra, y los hilos, y todo esto de hače por el Mapa que
tiene echo el Maestro. Para el estacado se dice que este ha de ser
segun el Dueño de la obra, porque pueden ir mui juntas las estacas,
o algo desapartadas. Las estacas son segun el terreno, si salen quatro
en Morillo se pagan cinco reales el ciento de su agusadura. Cada
carro carga 25 Morillos, y son de sedro. Cada uno vale 1½ reales

Title page of the original manuscript, *Architectura mechanica conforme la practica de esta Ciudad de México.*

fuera de el acarreo. Tienen de largo 6 varas. La agusadura de estos puede componerse con el carpintero de la obra.

Zepas de las Pilas. El cimiento de qualesquiera se llama Zepa: Señalado que sea, se abre la Zepa de tres, o quatro varas, conforme fuere el terreno, y la magnitud, y figura de la Pila, con advertencia, que hande ir mui unidas las estacas, luego se echa piedra dura con mescla de cimiento hasta que falta una vara para enrrasarse, toda aquella vara, o vara y media, para el enrrase se maziza con piedra dura y mescla de tesonclale, o mescla fina, hasta enrrazar.

Arena. Viene en Burros, o Mulas, cada Burro carga 12 o 16 costales, o 3 o 4 costales cada Mula. La mejor segun el Padre Fray Laurencio es la que Desarramada en la ropa no deja polvo, y segun otros laque refregada entre las manos no deja barro alguno. Viene de varias partes como de la Piedad, Tacubaya, Escapusalco, etc. Se compone por viages, y un viage de Arena es a conforme el cajon en que se recive por que dan 8 cajones por 4 reales y ai viage que dan los mismos 8 cajones por 5 reales.

Cal. Viene de varias partes. La mejor es la de San Marcos. La mas superior es aquella que hace mucho estrepito a el apagarla, y esta es la mejor para lechada. La cal se compone por carretadas, la carretada ha de tener 10 cargas, y cada carga ade tener 12 a 12 libras, y acada carga se le quitan 12 libras de tara.

Mesclas. La real: un huacal de cal, y otro de Arena. Mescla segunda uno de cal y dos de Arena. Mescla fina una de cal, y otro de Arena cernida: Si sale esta, o de esta medio cajon de granzas se le vuelve a echar, esse medio cajon de cal. Mescla de alplanar, uno de arena, y otro de cal, se rebuelbe primero y luego se cierne uno y otro. Mexcla terciada, o de cimientos prudencialmente 3 caxones de cal, 6 de Arena, y 12 de Tierra.

Piedra. Para mompostear hade ser dura, y se compone por brazas. La braza tiene 4 varas de largo, 2 de ancho, y una de alto: Su precio regular son quatro pesos.

Tesoncle. Con la misma medida de la piedra dura, se mide el Tesoncle, Las calidades de este que viene a Mexico, son dos, el de la Toya, que es duro, y el de la Barranca, que es blando. El blando vale seis pesos la brasada, y el duro cinco pesos. Ay brazadas de Tesoncle que llaman de laja, y media laja. La media laja es mayor que la laja. El precio de la laja, y media laja a veces 8 pesos, y avecs 12 pesos.

Canteria. Para labrar se divide en dos calidades frequentemente: en canteria, y chiluca, la canteria es menos dura que la chiluca, y viene de los Remedios, y otras partes, tiene cada atravesado, o piedra de canteria ⅔ de largo ½ vara de ancho y ¼ y dos dedos de grueso. Pisietes de canteria, o chiluca tienen ½ vara de largo, ⅓ poco mas de ancho, y una quarta de grueso; estos pisiestes valen la mitad de lo que vale el atravesado, cada atravesado vale de 3½ reales hasta 5 reales. Ay otro genero de piedra que llaman colorada, y esta solamente viene de Guadalupe.

Guijarro. Es piedra redonda dura que se trae solamente de Tacubaya, el viage es a cinco reales que son tres costales, los mismos que trae un viage de arena.

Ladrillo. El de marca tiene ⅓ de largo y de ancho ⅙ y el grueso tres dedos. El demas Ladrillo comun es de dos dedos de grueso, y cerca de una tercia de largo, y cerca de una sexma de ancho. Vale el grande 5 pesos 4 reales o 6 pesos el Millar, lo bueno de el se conoce por lo bien cosido. Quatro espicies ay de Ladrillo, que son recocido, recolorado, colorado, y naranjado, la primera y segunda calidad es bueno, las dos segundas inferiores. Buen Ladrillo viene de Tacubaya, de los Morales, Mixcasaque, Piedad, etc. menos el de Mexico, aunque es bueno para mampostear, y otras cosas.

Lozas. Estos se llaman tenayucas, y son de a vara, su precio es un real, pero esto no es regular; ay de ¾ ay de media vara, y ay de a ⅓.

Madera. Sirve para todo genero de obras, pero las principales son el oyamel, xalocote, sedro, y ocote; y comenzando por las Ystapalucas se dice que tienen 6 varas, quando menos, y de grueso, tres dedos, valen a tres reales. Siguense los quartones de a 7 varas de Oyamel, valen a tres, y medio reales. Quartones de a 8 varas, valen a quatro reales. Antepechos de a 6 varas: (En esto ay mandado, y ay Ordinario.) Lo mandado se dice por tener mas grueso que lo ordinario. Bigas de a 7 varas valen a siete reales. De a 8 varas a ocho reales (de estas ay ordinaio, y mandado). Bigas de a 9 varas a nueve, y a diez reales. Bigas de a 10 varas, de doze a cartoce reales. (En estas ay mandado, y ordinario.) Bigas de a 11 veras a dos pesos. Bigas de a 12 varas a diez y ocho, o veinte reales. Todo esto baja y sube de precio. Siguense las Planchas de sedro que son de a 5 varas y estas llamas lumbrales, y ay de a 6 varas de largo ½ vara de ancho, y ⅓ de grueso, y estas sirven para acerrar tablones: lo regular es que sean de Oyamel pero pueden ser de Xalocote etc. Lo ordinario que llevan los carretones de cada flete son 4 reales y cada flete es de quenta de el Dueño de la obra. Un carretón carga de Ystapalucas: 16. 8 quartones de a 7. 8 quartones de a 8. 6 Bigas de a 7 en carro. 4 Bigas de a 8. 3 Bigas de a 9 en carro. 2 Bigas de a 11 y 1 Biga de a 12 en carro. Un Lumbran en cada carro. Morillos de sedro 25 en Carro.

Tablas de techar y Tajamanil. Ay tres especies, unas son de Xalacote, que van a 2 reales dozena, otra de el Oyametal, o Chalco, estas valen a 3 o 4 reales dozena y tienen estos 1¼ varas de largo y ⅓ de ancho, y de grueso un dedo. Tablas de Ysclahuaca tienen 2 varas de largo ½ vara de ancho, y una pulgada de grueso, su valor es de 8 hasta 12 reales dozena. De dos maneras se ponen las tablas en los techos, ojuntadas, o traslapadas, de qualquiera manera que se pongan necesitan su cinta de taxamanil. La carga de Taxamanil se compone de 120 tajamaniles y vale a 2½ reales.

Hierro para fabricas se compone por libras. Barretas los mas grandes hande tener 19 libras calzadas de Azero por punta y voca, puede ajustarse cada libra de lo labrado a quatro reales con el herrero, o como se compusiere. Azadones ande tener de 5 a 6 libras, y no mas pesados, el mismo labrado ba de quenta del herrero, y lo mismo los rodadillos. Hierro de rexas, ventanas, corredores, pasamanos, etc. Si va de quenta de el Dueño hade comprar el Hierro, y puede pagar al Herrero siendo obra ordinaria a 7 y 8 pesos quintal, y ban de quenta de el Herrero las mermas; siendo la obra fina se llega ajustar por libras. Lo labrado de clavos de media naranja para puertas, es su valor de 2½ a 3 reales dozena. Alcayatas de 9 hasta 12 reales dozena: esto regularmente lo travajan en Juchimilco. Ay tambien Alcayatas de candado, de ventanas, de estantes, que se mandan hacer aproposito, y lo mismo lo demas que se ofrece como chapas, serrojas, etc.

Varios terminos de que usan los Maestros

El Taller viene aser la oficina de los canteros donde estos travajan = el Principal de ellos, que los raya alos otros, y esta puesto en lugar de el Maestro, se llama capataz.

Pies d.ⁿᵒˢ A ┊ Bazas â 5 r. l
Soclos B ┊ Pies d.ⁿᵒˢ â 4½ r.
Salmeres T ┊ Salmeres
Bazas Z ┊ vna quar
Sobre baza X ┊ tilla mas
Las que mⁱⁿᵃⁿ á ┊ con que
dentro O Mochetas ┊ vna

Las frentes A se llaman Paramentos.

c. Puerta se compone de Soclo ⅃ Feronele de vna quarta, soclo ⅃ Chilu
ca de vna ô dos Piedras segun el dueño de la Obra. Baza sobrebaza
⅃ Chilca, pies derechos de Cortexia summinexo, segun el claro
de la Puerta desde cinco Piedras, hasta once seg.ⁿ fuere el claro.

Llamasen soclos, Bazas, Pies derechos Serramientos, todo
esto ordinario. De todas estas especies ay ⅃ vna Namba que
llaman, ay ⅃ dos Nambas, ay moldados, acossinados, ay ⅃
moldura, ay ⅃ medio Chebe, acossinador, y moldados ⅃ mucho
buelo.

Las Puertas con sus Soclos, Bazas, y
sobrebazas, pies d.ⁿᵒˢ con la baza aticurga ⅃ diferentes acossinados,
y moldurai, como lo pide la obra composita, estas se van despues de el
Serramiento con su alquitrabe, friso, Cornisa, sus piedras ⅃ trigli
fos, Volutas, en estas Piedras ay diferentes por que vnas llaman
gramas, otras rincones, otras corridas, y otras con sus Ingleses.

La Linea dirá, y no la Lignea por.e es disparate.
Llamase area ala superficie que se mide, como si tubo vna p.ᵃ
ocho varas ⅃ largo, y quatro ⅃ ancho, se dirá que tubo treinta
y dos varas ⅃ area esto se entiende quadradas.

Práctica de rayar vna Puerta. Es esencialissimo
saver rayar vna Puerta, y por que saviendola rayar se saven los
terminos es como sigue: esto ba sin praⁿᵉ solo para exemplo
sea A B. el enxuxado de el Simiento fuera de el taluz donde
se ade rayar la Puerta A C. es el grueso que ade tener la Pa
red; Supongamos que la Puerta tiene dos varas de claro, con
que quedará segun esto, y se hara el Repartimiento como
se vee enfrente.

A page from the original manuscript.

El Tapial es el cerco de Madera, que se pone alas obras por recinto para que quede libre el paso de la calle, y queden dentro los Materiales de la obra.

Para rayar en la Pared las perpendiculares, hande ser a plomo y las paralelas Orizontales a nivel. *Catheto* = se llama la perdendicular que baja de arriba para abajo y no qualquier otra.

Michinales. Son los ahujeros que quedaron despues de haver puesto los andamios, conclida, y acavada la obra.

El Sardinel, es el quicio, o Umbral de la Puerta en el techo, de abajo de Mocheta, a Mocheta.

El Taluz, es lo que sobra de el Vivo de la Pared, por una y otra parte, sobre el enrrasado del cimiento, por que no estan ancha la Pared, quanto lo es el cimiento y esta sobra se llama Taluz.

Coluna: se llama, y no columna, que es impropriedad de el Arte.

Petril: se pronuncia y no Pretil que es locucion mui impropia.

Escantillon, es la medida de la cosa: es nombre general, y assi dar escantillon quiere decir dar el grueso de la Piedra, Biga, etc.

Una Danza de Arcos, o rayar una Danza de Arcos: quiere decir quando van muchos de ellos seguidos, bien por el un Costado, o por quatro etc.

Quebrantarse un techo: quiere decir quando tiene encima mucho peso, que le agovia, o quando se mira mui cargado, o mui vencido, se dice estar quebrantado.

Terraplenar: rigorosamente es llenar de tierra, pero se significa por terraplenar, mazizar, hinchir lo vacio etc.

Calafetear. Sucede en las Pilas, y en muchas Casas quando están rajadas se hace afuerza de Escoplo, con esparto rezina, y mescla fina.

Zenefa. Se llama, y no Zaneja como muchos con impropriedad la llaman.

Faena. Es el travajo que se expande de corto tiempo en una obra, principalmente en los dias festivos.

Adobe: ay dos calidades, una que se llama de marca, y otro de sancopinca: El de marca vale a 6 reales el ciento, y el de Sancopinca, a 5 reales.

Ripio. Viene como la Arena en Costales su precio es a medio la carga, o ados Cargas por real y medio.

Salarios de los operarios Albañiles

El oficial superior seis reales.
El oficial bueno cinco reales.
El medio cuchara quatro reales.
Peones tres reales en muchas partes dos y medio reales.
Cabritos uno y medio o dos reales.
Soquitero tres reales.

Dia de la Raya es el Savado por la costumbre, se la paga a cada operario su travajo revajando el real de comidas, que se les da entre semana.

El Empedrador oy dia tiene examen por quantos Ladrillos entran en una sala que tenga tantas varas de largo y tantas de ancho. Lo que al Maestro toca saver. El ajuste con estos es vario, pues ay a 2 reales vara quedrada, y se da caso que hagan vara a tres quartillas. Por los dos reales referidos ponen tierra y Peon, y ba de su quenta el empedrado; por un real y aun por tres quartillas se les hade dar la Tierra, y el Peon.

Pintores ay varios Maestros como pinturas. La azul es la mas corriente, su Zenefa, como de otros colores tienen diferentes precios, por que si se manda hacer de buen dibujo: ay de a quatro reales vara, y de tres reales si se manda hacer de menos dibujo ay de dos reales, de un real, de tres quartillas, y de medio real la vara. Ay zenefas que hacen a veinte varas por un peso, ay de a treinta, de a quarenta, de a cinquenta, y hasta sesenta varas por un peso; si se almagreá no mas, ay de un peso toda una pieza, o quatro reales y lo mismo accede quando se Jaspea. Si se ofrece que rayan pintadas algunas figuras o cavallo etc. a diez reales y hasta seis reales cada una.

Los Canteros, o travajan por dias, o a destajo, si por dias el Maestro hade veer si merecen a seis or siete reales, si adestajo, le ade pagar segun el conchavo de las piedras.

Pies derechos, *A.*
Soclos, *B.*
Salmeres, *T.*

Baza, *Z*.

Sobrebaza, *X*.

Los que miran adentro *O*, Mochetas.

Bazas a 5 reales, pies derechos a 1½ reales, salmeres una quartilla mas con que una.

Las Frentes *A* se llaman Paramentos. Puerta se compone de soclo de Tesoncle de una quarta, soclo de Chiluca de una o dos Piedras segun el dueño de la obra. Baza sobrebaza de Chiluca, pies derechos de canteria su numero, segun el claro de la Puerta desde cinco Piedras, hasta once segun fuere el claro.

Travajan soclos, Bazas, Pies derechos serramientos, todo esto ordinario. De todas estas especies ay de una xamba que llaman, ay de dos xambas; ay moldados, acojinados, ay de moldura, ay de medio reliebe, acojinados, y moldados de mucho buelo.

Ay Puertas con sus Soclos, Bazas, y sobrebazas, pies derechos con la baza aticurga de diferentes acojinados y molduras, como lo pide la orden composita, estas se usan despues de el cerramiento con sus alquitrabe, friso, cornisa, sus piedras de triglitos, volutas, en estas Piedras ay diferentes por que unas llaman esquinas, otras rincones, otras corridas, y otras con sus yngletes.

La Linea dirá, y no la Lignea por que es disparate. Llamase area ala superficie que se mide, como si tubo una pieza ocho varas de largo, y quatro de ancho, se dirá que tubo treinte y dos varas de area esto se entiende quadradas.

Practica de rayar una Puerta. Es esencialissimo saver rayar una Puerta, y por que saviendola rayar se saben los terminos es como sigue: esto ba sin pitipie solo para exemplo sea *AB* el enrrasado de el simiento fuera de el taluz donde se ade rayar la Puerta *AC* es el grueso que hade tener la Pared; Supongamos que la Puerta tiene dos varas de claro, con que quedan oi segun esto, y se hará el repartimiento como se vee enfrente.

Mocheta una quarta.

Tras dos una sexma.

Claro de la Puerta dos varas.

Derrames todo lo que da hasta el grueso de la Pared.

Frente de la Pilastra.

Otros Varios Terminos

La Lechada sirve para el blanqueó, se hace de Cal Viva la mas fina toda en piedra, y para hacerla se entierran oyas debajo de tierra por que con la fortaleza no se rebienten, poco a poco se ban apagando las piedras con la agua necesaria, y luego se deja apodrir la lechada = mientras mas podrida está mejor: la cal se hade escoger como arriba se dijo.

El Zulaque se compone de Cal, pelos de Chivato y manteca, a golpe, hasta que esto toma correa se doba y luego se hacen tablillas.

Rodapie es el contrasimiento que se le hace a una fabrica quando se quiere caer, y es porque le falta el grueso a el Simiento, entonces se hace un Contrasimiento encadenado que se llama rodapie, su grueso hade ser segun lo que pidiere la necessidad de el caso.

Padrino de la Pared se dice al Vivo de la Pared que va guardando una misma rectitud fuera de las molduras.

Cortina se llama un muro de mamposteria, o de canteria, no mui alto, que se labró para algunos fines, toda la vez que este siga derecho por un mismo paño se llama cortina.

Vara cubica de Pared, en Arquitetura significa el precio que se la ha regulado, y este sirve para las tasaciones, a este se le ha regulado valer tres pesos, y por otros veinte reales.

Cascajo es la Mescla vieja que ha servido en otra echatrosos pequeños, sirve la tierra la qual hade ir bien limpia para que no se crien ormigueros en la Azoteas.

Xalpaco se hace de Mescla aguada no mescla terciada, y sirve para antes de el blanqueo.

Regla para hazer las varas cubicas en una Pared

El Lienzo que se hade havaluar supongamos los Z tiene de altura 4 varas, el cimiento tenga 1½ varas, el largo sean 5 varas, y el grueso de la Pared sean ⅔. Esto medido sumese el simiento con la altura 4 y salen 5½ por toda la altura que ay desde el pie de el simiento hasta arriva multipliquese el largo 5 por el alto 5½ y salen 27½ estas 27½ multipliquese por el nominador del quebrado de el grueso que es 2 y salen 55. Estos 55 partanse al denominador 3 y salen varas cubicas 18⅓ havaluense al precio aque esta regulada la vara cubica, a tres pesos, o aveinte reales como se dijo, y se habrá hecho el havaluo.

Maximas para un Maestro

Nunca afecte terminos facultatibos delante de los operarios por que como no los entienden prorrumpen en riza, lo que havia de ser en alavanza, y assi sea regla general que para enseñarlos use de aquellas voces que usan ellos, diciendoles, ben aca hijo, coge tu palito, y essa vara, clavalo aqui, traite la regla, ponla aqui encima, ben, dá la buelta al rededor, etc. Este es el modo de conservarse para que los miren con respecto.

No se aparte jamas de lo que nos han escripto los Authores, por que ninguno puede decir mas que ellos: Hablo de los Maestros, el punto critico de la dificultad consiste en saver bien los elementos de geometria, arithmetica civil, y cortes de canteria, podrá meter la mano entre los mas abentajados Architectos, aunque los de esta Corte fundan su Magisterio, en los puntos mechanicos, no ay que hacer caso de estos pues al fin, y al cabo se rinden: Dado caso que los Authores no trageran lo que ellos llaman practica, pero como de todo se hace cargo como es constante, una vez que uno este fundamentado en las reglas generales, y principios referidos, puede echar a Monte atodos los que se quieren oponer contra justicia.

Modo de tirar una Pared sin que se caiga la de arriba que carga sobre la que se ade tirar

Sean los Paredes *A.B.* que la *B* carga sobre *A* le importa al Maestro tirar la Pared *A* para algunos fines: como avemos para tirarla sinque se sienta la de arriba. Operacion: en la Pared de arriba haganse unos ahujeros *L* y por estos entre los quartones *J* que descansen sobre el techo *J* y sus Bigas, que corran de *C* para *G* y lo mismo en la parte opuesta: Empiesese a tirar por *M* para que al mismo paso que se fuere ahujerando se vaya introduciendo la Biga *E.G.* que tenga el mismo escantillon que el grueso de la Pared *B* para que assi asiente con comodidad, y perfeccion. Digo ahora que aunque la Pared de abajo se tira, no aya miedo que caiga la de arriba.

Demonstracion. Los ahujeros *L* se han con la mescla, y piedra de tal suerte que vienen a ser como un mismo continente, por la travason de todas suspartes, o como una Boveda, luego si se introducen las Bigas J y se tira la pared A la pared B carga sobre macizo, esto es sobre las Bigas, y techo. Lo que puede obstar es, que como las partes Z no tienen substentaculo, por aqui pueden sentirse, digo a esto que es verdad; pero que como es mui corto el tiempo que assi se hande mantener, por que luego ba entrando la solera E aque descanze por iguales partes; no ay riesgo, y esto está provado.

Prosiguen las difiniciones

Ayre de una casa. No es otra cosa que lo que se puede fabricar sobre ella, este tambien se compra, y suele suceder ser una casa de dos Dueños: El suelo de uno y el Ayre de otro, aunque me parece que ay ordenanza para que las casas no puedan subir mas que auna medida prefixa, como se puede entender por las que estan construidas en esta Ciudad.

Mediania. No es otra cosa sino que una Pared pueda servir a las dos casas, si se hade fabricar, una junta a dos estas es en medio, deve pagar mediania, a entrambas, lo qual se deve asentar en las escripturas; y al vender qualquiera sitio Ayroso, se deve ver si entran las medianias por que entonces vale mas, que es el ahorro, que hade tener para fabricar su casa el que compra.

Alfardas son las Bigas inclinadas que se ponen para fabricar una Escalera, que no es de Bobeda, y a este genero de escaleras se llama de Alfardas.

El Divino Material se llama el Tesoncle por lo que agarra, y assi aunque los cortes de una Bobeda no baian con aquella perfeccion del Arte, son tolerables; no se dice por esto que las Bobedas, que se hacen en Mexico no tienen cortes por que se verá que esta imperfeccion la suplen los Yndios con hazer las piedras a manera de un Cucurucho mui largo, y mazizando bien por arriba parece un Puerco espín, por la travason de todas sus partes pero se deve creer, y entender que llevan cortes.

Partes de una Puerta Ordinaria

Las partes principales de que se compone una puerta son tres Cercos, Peinazos, y Peinazones. Cercos llaman los pies derechos donde atraviesan los Peinazos, y Peinazones, los de abajo que tambien se llaman caneros: las Bigas ahugeradas donde se mueve la puerta se llama chumasera, la quisialera es el macho, y el tejuelo de abajo la hembra, de Peinazo a Peinazo, quiere decir lo mismo que de clavos, a clavos, y estas son medianias.

Partes de un suelo embigado

Sobre el suelo immediatamente otra biesa la pieza un petril que se llama soclo, sobre este carga una biga que se llama solera: sobre la solera assienta una biga labrada que deje taluz por una, y otra parte para que carguen las bigas sobre la solera, estas bigas se llaman duelas, lo mismo que se adicho de en medio se hade entender por los Costados *XZ,* se mira descubierto para que se vea lo interior, por que sobre el taluz cargan las duelas, como se mira.

Malas costumbres de esta Arte

1. Firmar los Abaluos sin haver recivido el dinero, y como aveces es indespensable por no haver el dinero a causa de no haverse rematado la finca. Para esto no ay remedio.

2. Que saquen Angel, y que se Gremio, nacido todo esto de la omission, o ignorancia de los Maestros, y como ya está en costumbre, no se puede quitar.

3. Que el Maestro mayor de Real Palacio, le firme el Yngeniero las Memorias de lo que ha gastado para que el Virrey le dé las libranzas de lo que ha gastado, y diga que le paguen, pues hacer mui poca confianza de el Maestro mayor.

4. Que dichos Alarifes hagan a ojo las tazaziones, sin mas regla que la que les ha dado la experiencia de haver visto rematar las casas; esta no es regla, sino Juicio, que a veces puede llegar a temerario pudiendose valer de la regla dada en este numero, y de saver lo que puede valer una vara de techo embigado, y en ladrillado, etc.

5. El ser Maestro de una obra por tal qual regalo, y no visitarla, pues el Dueño, o quien está corriendo con la dicha obra, puede errar en mucho, y cargan sobre el Maestro, todas las barras de los otros en perjuicio de su credito.

6. Que todos los Maestros se titulen mayores, quando esto solo le es peculiar a el Maestro de las Reales Fabricas, de tal suerte que

por es lo tienen el titulo por el Rey, y deve entender en los examenes de los dhos, y demas cosas a el Arte anexas; El modo de firmarse los demas deve ser Fulano de tal Maestro de esta Nobilissima Ciudad y Fulano de tal Maestro de las obras del Santo Oficio combento etc.

Methodo y practica de hazer una Tazazion

Don Fulano de tal, Maestro mayor de la Nobilissima Ciudad y del Arte de Arquitectura en esta Nueva España, nombrando Perito para el reconocimiento, y habalue de una Casa, cita en terminos del barrio de la Alameda, por parte de los Muy Reverendos Padres del Hospicio de San Nicolas: Digo que haviendola registrado, y medid sufrente que corre de Oriente, a Poniente, hallo constar de cinquinta varas y su fondo que gira de Norte a Sur, hubo setenta y cinco varas usuales, Mexicanas, que respecto al parage en que se hallan, segun Pragmatica de esta Nobilissima Ciudad valen la cantidad de Doscientos cinquinta pesos: Assi mismo en dicho suelo se halla construida una fabrica de mamposteria ala moderna, que se compone de sala, Recamara, Assistencia, cozina, y otro quarto; todo competente, y los techos con sus derrames correspondientes, rexas, pasamanos, y ventanas, todo de fierro; Lo restante del citio esta ocupado con ocho quartos de a siete varas por quadro, y cada uno tiene dos Puertas la una que cae a dicho Patio de la Casa, y la otra aun corralito que sirve a beneficio de cada quarto, la qual Casa, como llevo expresado es de buena Mamposteria, y haviendo habaluado el Material, Rejas, Ventanas, Maderage, techos, y demas de el caso: Hallo valen juntamente con la cantidad del citio, la cantidad de cinco mil nuevecientos treinta y cinco pesos y assi lo declaro y Juro a Dios Nuestro Señor y ala Señal de la Santa Cruz por ser atodo a mi legal saver y entender y los firme, etc.—Fulano

Maestro mayor de el Real Palacio

[1.] Primeramente en lo primitibo tenia seiscientos pesos doscientos por el Real Palacio, y quatrocientos por la obra Material de la Santa Yglecia, hasta que en tiempo del Señor Ahumada, y Villalon, Virrey de esta Ciudad, vino una Real Cedula, para que el Juez de Obras (que siempre lo es un oydor, y sirve sin ningun estipen dio) suspendiera la obra del Real Palacio, y que en quanto al salario de el Maestro mayor fueran solos doscientos pesos, y que se lequitaran los quatrocientos de la Santa Yglecia, respecto a que los canonizos no havian pagado no se que ramo, lo qual assi quedo establecido.

2. El ir al Desague con los Virreyes, es solo politica, pro no es obligacion, solo del Maestro de la Ciudad.

3. Por la clausula del Titulo que dice que el Maestro mayor de Su Magestad y de las obras del Real Palacio goze de sueldo seis cientos pesos annuales, con los demas emolumentos, que le pertenecieren como atal. Por lo que dice a emolumentos, lo son cerraduras viejas, puertas, chapas, y demas maderas, y hierro viejo que se halle en la obra de su cargo, aunque esto se llegó a impedir por un Señor Virrey.

4. El Virrey dá los libramientos para que se le pague al Maestro mayor su Salario, con lo que huviere gastado.

5. El impertinencia de Maestro mayor pedir libramiento para veinte pesos que gasto: verbi gratia en un blanqueo, porque es mas lo que se gasta, que lo que se percibe, y assi se ba juntando hasta que ay cantidad notable.

6. Esto se dice respecto aque los Virreyes piden al Maestro cosas de poca monta y lo mismo las Señoras Virreinas, como que les blanquen una pieza Gavinete etc.

7. Si muere el Señor Virrey, y el Maestro no ha cobrado se pierde el dinero por que los oficiales Reales no pagan sin libramiento.

8. A Don Luis Navarro se le iban aperder quatro mil pesos y sino es por la Señora Doña Ynes que vino con Gracia Real, pierde el dinero, por que murio el Señor Virrey.

9. Ahora está mui gravada la plaza de Maestro mayor con solos doscientos pesos y es arbitro el oydor, o Juez de Obras aque le haga sus obras, se las visite, y mil impertinencias de valde.

Maestro mayor de la Ciudad

[1.] Primeramente este tal es elegido por los Regidores, y Diputados de ella, tiene su sueldo annual de trescientos pesos, con la obligacion de ir ala obra del Real Desague de Huehuetoca, con el Señor Juez del Desague en los tiempos competentes, que son al principio, o antes de las Aguas, o quando ay algun inmenite peligro en dicha obra.

2. No tiene mas emolumento que es al Salario que percive; y quando en los Caxones de la Plaza y Baratillo, se mudan Puertas, o se hace algun remiendo, tiene quatro reales de su Visita, y el cajonero le dá un par de Medias, u otra cosa de poca monta.

3. Tiene asu cargo Visitar todas las Obras pertenecientes a los propios de la ciudad sin sueldo alguno.

4. El Rexidor de Obras, es el que corre con todos, y con todos los Matheriales. El Maestro no se mete en otra cosa, que en visitar sus obras.

5. Tiene obligacion en los incendios yr a cortar el Fuego con Yndios, Barretas, y Cantanos.

6. Tiene obligacion de colectar nueve, o diez pesos de cada Casa de Pila que en algunas partes como San Andres dan Azucar; y este entero darlo al Rexidor de Obras para su destino, saluo si el Maestro saca o hizo postura a dicho asiento que entonces le puede quedar algo de las cañerias, y assi es solo assentista que dice.

7. Tiene mil Amos, como son el Correxidor, el Rexidor de Obras, y el Superintendente.

8. Tiene libertad qualquiera de los mencionados para sacarlo alas Vistas de ojos de quantos Acequias, Puentes, Calzadas, Cañerias, Ejidos, y todas las obras que pertenecen ala Ciudad.

Noticias

En Madrid el Maestro mayor tiene de sueldo cinco mil pesos Mexicanos, casa en el Real Palacio, Uniforme, Baston, y el Forlon de Camara. Por el Año de 1755 lo era Mozo que tenia 23 años.

La escultura, Pintura, y Architecctura, son las tres bellas Artes, en Virtud de las que en Paris, y en toda España asu titulo se ordenan.

De Cañerias

Ay mapa con la organizacion, y mutua complicacion que tienen entre si en lo subterraneo: Esto para el govierno y Policia de esta Ciudad, y para espender para ella sus Aguas. Su figura es a este modo verbi gratia A Caxa de Agua, y los demas son ramos en que se ba

dividiendo: la porcion de Agua que entra a esta Ciudad por los Caños de Chapultepeque, que es la mejor Agua, y viene de santa Fee,
la otra Agua que entra por los caños de Belen es mas gordita, y de
menos gusto y esta viene de la Alberca de Chapultepeque, cuyo serro
es amano, y sirve de sobre Alberca, para que no se espanten las
Aguas: Es obra de los Yndios Reyes de la gentilidad; ya se ha conocido merma en la Alberca y se ha calafetado.

Advertencias sobre algunos Cosas

En el punto de Estacas, hade saver el Architecto, que lo que
pudre no es el Agua sino, el Ayre: se experimenta en ellas, allandose
en algunos simientos indemnes despues de muchos años, y aquellas
partes que estan descubiertas, o enterradas, y en alguna parte descubiertas: El pedaso que esta defuera tiene la caveza podrida todo lo
que descubre por la corruccion de los Ayres.

En Supocicion de que un Oficial aya echo el dia de oy pongo
por Exemplo dos varas: Si estas se enrradaran; y se midieran mañana
se hallara que le falta tres, o quatro dedos por lo que asienta, con-
sume, y chupa el Matherial, como el Suelo en que estriba la Pared.

He oydo decir que quando se saca la Planta de un Templo, ha-
deser de suerte que la Puerta principal mire al Occidente por no se
que Rito de la Yglesia, lo qual se hara quando commodamente se
pueda, como es en lugares, que puede dar lugar el terreno, por no
tener fincas que lo impidan, por que si las ay la necessidad hara que
se fabrique como se pueda.

Obras de Talla y Piedra: Portadas

Llaman obras de Talla a las Portadas que ahora estan usando, y
verdaderamente no vienen aser otra cosa que unos colaterales en la
calle. El orden que hade aguardar el Architecto hade ser el siguiente.
La Planta de una portada bien lo puede hacer qualquier pintor
siendo diestro, pero este hade ser bajo aquel repartimiento que le
diere el Maestro verbi gratia los tamaños que le corresponde al primero segundo cuerpo etc. Mejor juzgue que dicha Planta o como
otros dicen el alzado lo aya de sacar un Maestro de Ensamblador.
Ensambladores son quellos artifices de colaterales: Dicese pues que

estos saven mui bien lo que es alzado, y las molduras que pueden entrar las boladas, y prosecturas quanto hande tener en todo lo demas que deve registrar, y corregir el Architecto antes de comenzar la obra, por que si save dibujar, vista la planta que le trae el Ensamblador. Veera si es agradable ala Vista y si tiene algunos defectos que corregir verbi gratia que le falte proporcion ala Cornisa, que los pedestales se reduzgan a aquel orden que deven tener por que ya se veé que es importante que cargue lo cano sobre lo Diorico, y otras cosas a este tener: corregida la planta, y haviendo salido a toda su contemplancion, llamará a los talladores sobre piedra y con el capataz de los canteros conferirá todo lo combeniente para dar principio asu obra que esten travajando arreglados ala planta de prespectiva, e ichonografica sin exeder los limites de lo que ha mandado el Maestro.

Ingletes. Son una moldura que no corre seguida sino que quiebra haciendo el angulo saliente con la misma moldura con que viene corriendo la Baza.

Zepas, es nombre no mui generico pues solamente cabe en algunos casos verbi gratia para hacer una Pila se abre Zepa, esto es su sanja; para hacer una escalera de bobeda, se abren zepas para donde hande ir los estribos; para hacer un Puente se abren zepas, y no se dice abrir simientos, sino abrir zepas.

Bolzores ha de decir el Maestro pero no Bolsones. Es termino de la canteria y assi me remito alos tratados de Montea, por lo que aqui se pone es lo que no esta en Libros de Architectura.

Andamios por savido se save loque son, pero si se advierte que tanto ganan al dia los oficiales: en ponerlos quanto pudieran travajando en la mamposteria.

Prueba del mamposteado: Echar cantaros de Agua ala Pared para veer si se resume, y sale por las yndiduras de lo mal travajado: Esta es falza ami veer.

Problema fuerte de los Maestros es dada una Pilastra que tiene 1⅔ vara de alto, y ⅔ de largo. Pidese con quantos pisietes que tienen tanto de largo, tanto de ancho, y tanto del grueso: Se puede construir.

Se advierte que los Alvañiles asi como mas ahondar deven ganar por que crese mas el travajo. De la misma manera quanto mas sube la obra deven ganar por la misma razon. Mirar a Tosca al fin del tomo primero de Mathematica.

Maestros de los Combentos

Cada combento de Monjas paga su Maestros annualmente: unos dan cien pesos cana año, otros mas, y otros menos, aya lo que huviera que hacer, corren estos Maestros con las Casas, Obras, aderezos, y remiendos de celdas, y todo lo que se ofrece hacer, las vistas de ojos, Tazaciones de Matheriales, y registrar las celdas de las Monjas. A el Maestro le paga el Mayordomo de el combento; aunque el Maestro no corre con las quentas de el Matherial, sino solamente firmar las Memorias de el Mayordomo. Ay algunos combentos donde el Maestro pone sobre estante asu satisfacion y corre con las quentas de cal y Matheriales, y en una palabra todo el dinero pasa por su mano, pero lo regular es que el Mayordomo corre con todo esto, y el Maestro solamente firma, y jura las Memorias de lo que ha gastado, pero aqui entra el gravisimo escrupulo del Maestro, por que aunque el Mayordomo sea mui fiel como este se vale de el sobre estante, y el sobre estante puede en lugar de poner quatro carretadas de cal, poner cinco o seis, de aqui nace que el pobre Maestro nunca puede jurar las Memorias sin que pase el gasto por su mano. El Señor Doctor Don Manuel Rubio, y Salinas, quiso saver en que se consumian las rentas de los combentos, llamó a el Maestro Mayor Don Miguel Espinosa de los Monteros, para que lo fuera de todas las obras de su filiacion y par diez, que por haver querido los Mayordomos que firmara y jurara las Memorias, dejó este Emolumento dando por causa que no podia jurar lo que no havia visto, y que para que lo jurara era menester correr con la raya y todos los demas pagamentos de Matheriales.

Examen de un Architecto

1. Que el examinado deve comparecer ante los Veedores del Arte para que se cercieren de su Ydoneidas.

2. Dicho Examinado no es menester aya Sido Sobre estante, hasta que sea practico, e inteligente en el Arte, y este es punto Executoriado como, atestigua, la comun practica nacido de cierto litis.

3. Como ni tampoco que sean las ordenanzas que se hande seguir las mismas, que trae el Padre Fray Lorenzo en su Architectura sino las Patricias que estan en Cavildo.

4. Los Veedores de el Arte deven asignar dia para el Examen a contento de el Examinado, este puede ser en qualquiera Casa particular.

5. Constara el Examen de dos partes. Una mañana y una tarde consecutibas, la tarde para el Taller y la Mañana para la obra.

6. El examen sobre el Taller se reduce a la Geometria practica, Algebra, Architectura, y Cortes de Canteria, y estos tratados puede haver Visto en el Padre Tosca, menos la Architectura que podra veer en Uvolfio pues no deja piedra por mober.

7. El examen de la obra se reduce aque asiento una Pilastra o un tramo de Corniza, o otra cosa mecánica, que deve hacer son sus proprias manos, para que de esto aya de dar fee el Escrivano de Cabildo.

8. Pueden los Maestros en este caso hazerlo rayar qualquiera arco, o genero de bueltas en la Pared, y esto acavado se presenta en Cavildo, para que le libre el titulo suficiente que se llama Carta de Examen: Pagara assimismo de media annata 12 pesos 4 reales y demas gastos de oficio. Llegan los gastos del titulo y funcion de tarde y mañana a poco mas or menos de 100 pesos.

9. Ay examen de lo blanco, y examen de lo prieto: Examen de lo blanco se entiende para hacer tazaciones, y poder correr con las obras de mamposteria, y canteria. Examen de lo prieto, solo se entiende para obras de abode, y que solo pueden servir en las obras, de lo mismo que un oficial, pero no para hazer las tazaciones de Provincia. etc. y como suelen decir es un examen, que se le confiere aqualquiera Albañil, aunque no sepa leer, y escrivir.

10. Tazaciones las puede hallar el Maestro en la Audiencia de abajo que alli se hacen muchas, por las razones de remate.

11. En el Juzgado de Capellanias ay mucho que hacer; pero este Juzgado tiene su Maesto particular.

12. En la Real Audiencia ay pocas tazaciones por que por experiencia consta lo poco que ay que hacer.

13. Finalmente ninguna tazacion sirve sino es, firmada de Maestro examinado, y este es buen regimen, por que regularmente los Alcaldes Mayores en las fianzas de el Rey dan sus fincas que ponen sus Fiadores para seguro de los tributos, y los papeles y escrituras llenan tazacion del Maestro para que sepa el Rey lo que vale la casa, y assi el menester que baya el habaluó por Maestro examinado.

Ynstrumentos y Libros que ha de tener un Maestro

Primeramente par cartilla un compendio Mathematico por el Padre Tosca: Estudiara los Elementos de Euclides en el mismo orden que alli se hallan, si quiere despues con los de mas tratados hasta haver visto el tratado de Architectura Militar por servir de mucha luz a el tratado de Architectura Civil, y Cortes de Canteria.

Ytem. Un Juego de Serrano de Astronomia Unibersal pues aunque no sirve ala Architectura trae alo ultimo un tratado de geometria espaciosa mui Essencial a el Architecto para quedar bien en sus funciones.

Ytem. Un Juego de el Padre Fray Laurencio que escrivio de la architectura, pues aunque esta obra respecto a el corto tratado que escrivió el Padre Tosca no sirve, pero da mucha luz para entenderlo y da muchas noticias, y sobre todo enseña los terminos y material lenguaje de los Maestros.

Ytem. Un Uvolfio por lo que escrivió de Architectura es tan especial que no ay mas que desear en la materia: Excrivio de Argamasas, y de otras practicas, que no se hallan en otro Author.

Ami me parece que estos Authores sobran para un Maestro. Los Ynstrumentos que hade tener son los siguientes. Para delinear los Mapas que no se suman las puntas del Compaz tendra una plancheta de firme bien lisa y si pudiere ser de broma será mejor, y que tenga por lo menos de largo, y ancho mas de media vara.

Ytem. Un Estuche con todos sus piezas y el Uso de la Pantrometra lo verá en el Padre Tosca.

Ytem. Un Nibel de Madera bien echo y Capaz con sus plomada, todo mui curioso y tratable.

Ytem. Los Mapas siguientes. El Mapa de las Aquas que anda impreso, y escrito por Don Carlos de Siguenza para que se actué en todas las corrientes circumbencias de esta Ciudad.

Ytem. El Mapa de los precios: Esta Mapa no esta levantado emprespectiva, sino que solamente esta Planta Ychonographica para que pueda hacer las tazaciones.

Ytem. El Mapa de prespectiva de la misma Ciudad. Este solo sirve de curiosidad, pero adorna el Gavinete y arriba llevara la Ymagen de Nuestra Señora de Guadalupe con las Armas de Mexico. Este Mapa acompaña el otro.

Ytem. El Mapa de las Cañerias que arriva se dijo para que pueda veer donde cabe, o no cabe Merced, y que sepa dar razon de lo interior de los Cañerias con sus Saltos, y demas corrientes a el ramo de Aguas.

Estos son los Mapas principales. Fuera de estos ay otros principales, y son del todo este Reyno con lugares, Villas, y Ciudades: Escripto por Villa Señor, que anda impreso: trae hasta lo descubierto de Californias, y aunque esta echo mui abulto, pero da mucha luz para la inteligencia del Reyno.

Ytem. Un abujon para los Suelos y que sirva de Relox de Sol: Deve saver delinear los quatro Reloxes Verticales, por que se ponen en las Azoteas de los Collegios, y Casas particulares. Los podrá delinear haviendo visto el noveno tomo del Padre Tosca en el tratado de Geometria.

Ytem. Papel de Marca, y Pergamino para la delineacion de las plantas de las casas, y aqui que advertir al Maestro lo siguiente.

1. Que se pinte de colores los Vestigios de el enrrasado.

2. Que lo que es descanzo de Escalera se pueda distinguir de lo que es planta de ellas, como en el presente caso la planta de un descanso, se notara con los deaganales *A.B.C.* = de la planta de la Escalera vista desde arriba, se notara con el numero de Escalones, que se mira *B.E.F.* La distancia de una, a otro escalon, que son las paralelas, se llaman huellas, mire adelante endonde se trata de la formacion de una Escalera.

3. En los Mapas el enrrasado se manifestara con paralelas, como se mira, dandoles las mismas dimensiones que hade llevar el grueso de la pared y distancia de puertas, con mochetas, trasdos, y derrames como se podrá advirtiendo, que acada pieza se le hade poner el nombre de lo que assi: Bobega, Cochera, Asesoria, etc.

Ygualmente el Maestro tendrá Esquadra cordeles para sacar aplano y recto qualquier sitio, y por lo consono de este Arte con el oficio de Agrimensor tendra su Nibel de Agua con su pie, un Relox de péndola, y campana para el gavinete y una Muestra mui fiel para las diligencias de campo.

Ytem. Un buen abujon con su triangulo filar con la escala Geometrica todo esto hade tener: su meza a tres pies portatil y commobiniento libre a el oriente; tenga cordeles, vara de medir marcada por el fiel de esta ciudad la qual hade ir dividada y con esto me parece tiene bastante para el desempeño de su obligacion, salvo se quiere obserbar, y sequir la linea Mathematica que ya entonces necesita de otros instrumentos, pero ahora basta lo dicho.

Cathalogo de las obras publicas que en esta Ciudad pertenecen a los Maestros

1. Obra del Real Desague de Huehuetoca.
2. Obra de los Arcos de Chapultepeque.
3. Obra de el Real Palacio.
4. Obras de la Santa Yglecia, y Sagrario.
5. Obras de el Estado y Marquesado del Valle.
6. Obras de la Nobilissima Ciudad.
7. Obras de el Santo Oficio.
8. Obras de Cañerias.
9. Limpias de Ciudad y sus Acequias.
10. Reconocimiento de quintos, egidos, y Puentes circumbecinas.
11. Reconocimiento de Corrientes y vertientes.
12. Obras de los Combentos.
13. Vistas de ojos, y remates de los Juzgados.
14. Tasaciones generales, y particulares.
15. Obras de particulares.

Dictamenes que suelen dar los Maestros

Se acostumbra que quando ay algun punto dificultoso, sobre alguna obra, assi de los construidas como de otras que se pretenden construir ban los Maestro alas vistas de Ojos. Es importante asignar por menor lo que se puede ofrecer pero aqui seda el methodo general para que responda el Maestro. Esta respuesta se llama dictamen, o parecer del Maestro: se reduce aque el explique el orden methodo y progreso de la diligencia, que se practicó, si es obra de Calzada, hará el calculo de lo que ade costar. Si es conducto de Agua, despues de haver nibelado verá los parages por donde hade pasar el Agua, y dirá Verbi gratia que en tal parage hade pasar por Sanja de Cal y Canto, por lo poroso de la tierra, y que en tal distancia vaian 20 y mas arcos, y que de aqui atal parte puede ir en Sanja abierta con todo lo demas, que se fuere ofreciendo, y tenga gran cuidado en lo que se fuere ofreciendo de obra en los trechos para que despues no se cargue a su quenta: Dará assi mismo las medidas que obserbe, pondrá los fundamentos que tiene para que se haga, o no se haga, todo esto mui alo largo = si se cae, o quiere caer algun Templo, pondrá sus reparos, y la obra, que cave para que no se venga abajo = recurrira a las reglas de la estática, mirando hacia que parte gravita la fabrica, hará su demonstracion diciendo que si le carga peso asia tal parte hade caer, y que el Rodapie lo aya de tener no este lugar, sino en el otro, hará su demonstracion con lineas para satisfacer a las partes, si se ofreciere dar dictamen sobre puntos de aqueductos, si hande ir Subterraneos dara la medida de las formas, a el Mayordomo, o Administrador de las Haziendas de Campo para que este las mande fabricar de barro: quiero decir que dará el diametro de la cañeria con el grueso que viene a ser como dos circulos consentricos como se mira en esta figura, se pone el methodo pero el Maestro deve dar la Medida: Si era en punto de Alcantarilla vea quantos son los Ynteresados, y de quenta de quien hande ir los gastos, vea assi mismo la merced de cada uno para dar las medidas de los organos en la presente figura, se pone un Caso, y la planta de la Alcantarilla de la santissima Trinidad que ay quatro interesados, assi como se mira hade ir la superficie de la Alcantarilla los foramenes *A.B.C.D.* Son Organos que bajan al suelo para dividirse *A* es la merced de la Pila Real. *B* Baño de la Santisima. *C* Baño de Santa Tereza, y *D* Pila de San Lazaro y Santa Cruz.

En las Tasaciones
observará el Maestro lo Siguiente

1. Llevará en su Compania a un Yndio Albañil para que mida la frente, y el fondo de la casa que se ade hade habaluar, y si le parece lleve otro compañero para que le escriba la Tazacion, y sus Apuntes.

2. Llevará un Libro de los que llaman de Memorias con su Lapis.

3. Escrivirá para donde corren las paredes de fondo y frente, si

de Oriente a Poniente, o de Norte a Sur y es de adventir que en una tazacion entran lo Quatros vientos.

4. Ponga los nombres de las casas colindantes, o de sus Duen-ños, Plazuelos, y señas de el parage.

5. Haga un breve diseño parado alli de la planta de la casa, assi de su suelo como de su Ayre.

6. Vea si tiene mediania para que pueda añadir, o restar a la quenta segun lo dicho.

7. Rexistre las bigas de los suelos, y de los Techos, punzandolos para saver si estan podridas, y los Tabiques, y paredes haga tocar con alguna cosa maziza para veer si son de adove.

8. Finalmente reconosca mejores haciendo resumen de todas las oficinas, Calcule el Hierro por libras, o por arrobas, u quintales, se-gun fuere lo labrado; vea la vara de techo lo que viere util, y haviendo echo regulacion de la vara cubica de Pared segun el parage hará la Tazacion.

Extracto de Varios Citios con sus precios pero para el puntual conosimiento Siempre Ocurrira el Maestro al Mapa

Portales de los Mercaderes. 80 reales.

Casas de el Estado. 74 reales.

Calle de Santo Domingo Primera. 48 reales. Segunda. 58 rea-les. Tercera para salir a la Cruz de Tabarteros. 64 reales.

Real Aduana. 48 reales. Esquina de la Ynquicicion y su Calle. 24 reales.

Calle de la puerta falsa de Santo Domingo. 20 reales.

Puente de Santo Domingo. 18 reales. Bajado el Puente. 18 rea-les.

Portals de Santo Domingo. 32 reales. Plazuela del Combento. 18 reales.

Calle a el Oeste de Santa Catharina. 8 reales.

Esquina de Santa Catharina. 8 reales. Buelta al Sur. 12 reales.

Callejon que va a Santa Catharina. 6 reales. En su ultima dis-tancia. 8 reales.

Quadra antes de Santa Catharina Martir. 6 reales.

Plazuela de Santa Catharina. 8 reales.

Señora Santa Anna. ½ y tambien un real.

Puente al sur internandose a la Ciudad. 4 reales.

Quadra que sigue antes al Puente de Santo Domingo. 12 reales.

Torsiendo aqui a el oeste por detras de Santo Domingo. 12 reales.

Sigue Acequia por detras de la Misericordia. 8 reales.

Calle de tras de San Lorenzo. 8 reales.

Calle de San Francisco hasta la Esquina de Echavarri, y buelta. 80 reales.

Frente de San Francisco. 32 reales.

Quadra que se le sigue: su esquina. 35 reales.

La otra donde termina. 46 reales.

La que esta antes de la Professa. 56 reales.

Frente de la Professa. 56 reales.

Quadra que sigue. 64.

Esquina de las Brigidas, y Puente de San Francisco. 24 reales.

Frente de las Brigidas. 16 reales.

Esquina frente de Santa Ysavel. 30 reales.

Portales de las Tlapelerias. 80 reales. Su frontera. 80 reales.

Esquina de la Calle de la Palma. 58 reales.

Calle del Espiritu Santo. 42 reales.

Portales hasta el Coliseo Viejo. 42 reales.

Hasta el Nuevo. 36 reales.

Calle del Nuevo. 36 reales.

Collegio de Niñas. 24 reales. Su esquina frente de la Pila. 32 reales.

De alli para el Oriente. 48 reales.

Esquina de el Angel. 48 reales.

Calle de Capuchinas. 48 reales.

Desde alli su Esquina donde estava la Ymprenta de Hogal. 52 reales.

Calle de la Monterilla. 72 reales.

Calle de San Bernardo. 54 reales.

Plazuela del Bolador. 72 reales.

Real Universidad. 48 reales.

Calle que sigue a Portaceli. 40 reales.

Rejas de Balbanera. 40 reales.
Puente de el Correo Mayor. 40 reales.
Calle de quarteles. 40 reales.
Calle de la Merced. 40 reales. Hasta su Esquina. 32 reales.
Frente de la Merced. 24 reales.
Esquina del Puente alli. 20 reales.
Bajado el Puente. 6 reales.
Puente de Manzanares. 4 reales.
De alli asta la Lamedita. 2 reales.
San Lazaro a medio.
Desde aqui a el Oeste. Puente de Pacheco, y Pila. 1 real.
Bajado el Puente. 2 reales.
Quadra que sigue al mismo viento. 4 reales.
San Juan de Dios. 8 reales.
Santa Veracruz. 12 reales.
Caja de el Agua Puente de la Mariscala. 16 reales.
Calle de San Andres primera. 18 reales.
Segunda Frente de los Bethelemitas.
Calle de Santa Clara primera. 32 reales. Segunda idem.
Calle de Tacuba. 40 reales.
Esquina que sigue de la misma. 56 reales.
Alcaycería enfrente al Leste, son las Casas del Estado, Esquina
    de Tacuba, 74 reales. Y hasta llegar alos Portales al Sur. 80
    reales.
Calle de la Azequia. 40 reales.
Calle de Jesus Maria. 32 reales.
Puente de la Leña. 20 reales.
Bajado el Puente al Leste. 6 reales.
Calle de la Pulqueria de Pacheco, digo de Palacio. 4 reales.
Hasta Santa Cruz. 2 reales.
Resintos de este Barrio. A ½ y a 1 real.
Puesto en Monzerrate. 8 reales.
Detras de San Geronimo al Norte. 8 reales.
Calle que sigue. 8 reales.
Ala de Alfaro. 22 reales.
Esquina de San Augustin. 24 reales.
Calle que sigue. 32 reales.
Esquina de el Angel. 48 reales.

Calle hasta el Puente del Espiritu Santo. Entre 48 y 50 reales.

Calle de Espiritu Santo. 55 reales.

Calle de la Profesa al Sur. 40 reales.

La que sigue entre 28 y 40 reales.

La que sigue al Sur, entre 28 y 18 reales.

La que sigue 16 reales hasta un costado de Santo Domingo. 12 reales. que llaman Pila Seca.

Puesto en el Salto del Agua para la Concepcion al Norte.

Salto del Agua. 6 reales.

Quadra que sigue. 12 y lo mismo toda la calle derecho de San Juan hasta el Hospital Real.

Santa Isabel. 30 reales.

Caja de Agua. 18 reales.

Concepcion. 8 reales.

Frente de la Concepcion al Oeste. 2 reales.

Barrio de San Juan de Dios, San Hipolito, y Santa Vera Cruz. A 2 reales y 4 reales segun las fronteras de suerte, que las principales son a 4 reales, las internas a 2 reales y la Abarrada al Norte a ½ real.

Puesto en un lugar de Regina hasta San Lorenzo.

Plazuela, y Pila. 10 reales.

Puente de la calle de los Mesones. 16 reales.

Calle que sigue. 22 reales.

La que sigue. 24 reales hasta el Collegio de Niñas, y Calle del Coliseo Nuevo. 36 reales.

La que sigue. 32 reales.

La otra al Norte como hemos venido. 24 reales.

La que sigue. 8 reales.

Hasta San Lorenzo. 8 reales.

Puesto en la Parrochia de San Sevastian hasta la Puerta falsa de Santo Domingo.

En este Barrio a ½ real.

Quadra que sigue, y da buelta para el Carmen. 4 reales.

La que sigue al Deste. 6 reales.

La otra hasta la Puerta falsa. 6 reales.

Puesto en San Sevastian a espaldas de San Gregorio aqui al Deste a 4 reales.

Esquina de esta quadra. 6 reales.

Calle que sigue. 7 reales.

Calle que sigue, hasta Puente del Oriente se Santo Domingo. 8 reales.

Mochas su Albarrada interior, a ½ real.

Monzerrate su Albarrada interior, a ½ real.

A Orilla del Agua asta 3 reales.

San Antonio Abad, San Anton Tepito. A ½ real.

Obrage de San Pablo, Molino de Tablas. ½ real.

Albarrada de la Azequia, y Pipis a ½ real.

Queda la orilla de la Azequia hasta el Puente de los Curtidores que sigue a Norte desde 1 real hasta la Merced que vale 20 reales.

En la Pulqueria de Santo Thomas, desde aqui hasta el Puente de Santhiaguito. 3 reales en dicha Pulqueria. A ½ real.

Albarrada de la Palma, y ornillo, a ½ real.

Albarrada de Santa Cruz, a ½ real.

La de San Lazaro: a ½ real.

La de San Sevastian a ½ real mas retirado, a ¼ real.

Santa Cruz Acatlan. A ½ real.

Barrio de Santa Anna, a ½ real.

Barrio de San Thiago a ½, ay con Agua proporcionalmente.

Barrio de Santa Maria, a ½ real.

Detras de Casa de Concha, a ½ real.

Quadra que sigue, que es respaldo ala Santisima Trinidad. 12 reales.

En su esquina al mismo viento. 12 reales.

Para llegar a el Hospicio. 16 reales.

Calle de el Hospicio. 28 reales.

Esquina del Hospicio. 26 reales.

Calle de Santa Thereza la antigua. 32 reales.

Puente de Solano. 4 reales.

Quadra que sigue. 6 reales.

La que sigue asta Jesus Maris. 8 reales.

Estampa de Jesus Maria. 14 reales.

Calle cerrada del Parque. 20 reales.

Buelta al Norte. 32 reales.

Calle de Santa Ynes al Leste. 24 reales.

Calle del Amor de Dios. 24 reales.

Callejon del mismo al Leste. 18 reales.

Quadra que sigue hasta la Santisima Trinidad. 14 reales.

Quadra del Collegio, y Puerta falsa. 8 reales.

Quadra que sigue. 4 reales.

La de Pacheco. 2 reales y Hasta el Puente. 1 real.

Plazuela que sigue. ½ real.

Estando en San Juan de la Penitencia. Su Plazuela, al Norte. 5 reales.

La que igue al oeste. 4 reales.

Adelante a este viento. 2 reales.

Una quadra al deste. 1 real.

Arboles, y Albarrada al deste. ½ real.

Haziendo centro en San Juan sus Callejones al sur, el primero 3 reales.

El segundo a 2 reales.

El tercero a 1 real.

El cuarto. La Plazuela de los Caños al Norte. ½ real.

Centro en San Juan, a el Leste su Plazuela. 6 reales.

Calle de San Juan a este Viento. 12 reales.

Quadra Segunda que sigue a el Leste. 16 reales.

Calle de San Phelipe Neri. 22 reales.

Su Esquina. 24 reales.

Esquina de la calle del Arco. 24 reales.

Calle del Arco. 24 reales.

Al salir de la Calle de Jesus y hasta al Norte. 48 reales.

Calle de Jesus al Leste. 32 reales.

Plazuela de Jesus al Leste. 32 reales. Al Norte. 48 reales.

Calle del Parque del Conde al Leste. 16 reales.

Quadra de Jesus, al Leste. 12 reales.

Calle de Posadas. 10 reales.

Quadra que sigue su Esquina. Primeva a 8 reales.

La otra, a 6 reales.

En el Puente, a 6 reales.

Bajado este Puente al mismo viento a 3 reales.

Plazuela de la Palma. A 2 reales.

Albarrada, a ½ y a ¾ reales.

Como sigue a ½ real.

Frontero de las Mochas, a ½ real.

Belem de Mercenarios, a 2 reales.

Una quadra al Leste, a 3 reales.

Salto del Agua. 4 reales.

Para el Leste mas adentro. 8 reales.

Calle Real que mira rectamente al Collegio de San Pablo.

Plazuela del Salto del Agua. 8 reales.

Calle Real que sigue. 8 reales.

La que sigue al Leste. 8 reales.

Calle de Monserrate. 8 reales.

Monzerrate, y Espaldas de San Geronimo. 8 reales.

Calle detras de San Miguel. 8 reales.

Quadra que sigue hasta llegar ala Pila de San Pablo, y Esquina.
8 reales.

Plazuela. 6 reales.

Quadra que sigue. 4 reales.

Hasta llegar al Puente. 4 reales.

Como sigue orilla de la Azequia. 2 reales.

Albarrada a ½ real.

Plazuela de el Carmen al oeste. 4 reales.

Esquina de la Casa de el Estado, alli 74 reales.

Buelta Calle de Tacuba. 64 reales.

Escalerillas. 64 reales.

Calle del Relox.

Calle de los Cordobanes. 40 reales.

Puesto en el Salto del Agua como que ba ala Piedad y Calzada.

Quadra primeva. 6 reales.

Ultima, antes del Puente y Garita. 2 reales.

Puesto en San Fernando. ¼ real.

Siguese San Hipolito. 1 real.

Quadra hasta San Juan de Dios. 4 reales.

Quadra donde está la casa de Concha. 2 reales.

La que se afrenta en San Diego. 3 reales.

La que se afrenta ala Alameda. 4 reales.

En Corpus Christi. 5 reales.

Barrio de la Santa Vera Cruz, San Juan de Dios, San Hipolito,
y San Fernando, El Viento interior al Noroeste, es a ½ real
mas afuera a ¼ real.

Egido de Concha y Horca recinto en cortorno, a ¼ real.

Detras de Corpus Christi. Hasta 2 reales.

Estando aqui la Albarrada al sudueste a ½ real y mas retirado ¼.

Puente de los Gallos, o Esquina a espaldas de la Concepcion a el Sur. 8 reales.

Como sigue al oriente detras de San Andres, a 13 reales hasta acaba la quadra 18 reales.

Quadra que sigue al Leste desde 24 a 28 reales.

La que sigue desde 32 a 40 reales.

Desde aqui hasta esquina de Santa Thereza, hasta 12 reales.

En San Camilo su frente toda ella. 12 reales.

En San Joseph de Gracia de 12 a 20 reales.

Puestos o restituidos a los Portales de Santo Domingo desde la Encarnacion su Calle 26 reales. La que sigue al Deste que es de Bergara desde 32 a 24.

Se notara que faltan muchas calles en este Extracto y que las que estaban asignadas estan salteadas, pero ya queda advertido que el Maestro occurra al Mapa fuera de que en precios por los mismos tiempos variaran.

Todo lo demas de el ambito exterior de la Ciudad, se regula como tierras de Pastos.

Poniendo una caballeria de tierra en cinco mil pesos que es lo mas que puede valer, siendo de riego; sale la vara de tierra amenos de un octabo.

Architectura, civil, es una ciencia que enseña aplantar y edificar con firmeza, proporcion, y hermosura; Sus profesores aunque regularmente se equibocan con los nombres de Architectos, Alarifes, y Maestros Mayores, pero estrecha y rigorosamente se deven llamar Architectos y Maestros Mayores de tal: segun la obra que tienen asu cargo, como de Cuidad, Real Palacio, Santo Oficio, etc.

El Architecto, segun el sentido rigoroso de la Ley, es el Principe de los Edificios, o fabricas, llamase Principe, o principal, por ser el principal Edificator, que de las plantillas de los Arcos Bobedas etc. No es menester que sea de profession Albañil, como quieren algunos: basta que sea practico, en la Architectura, Montea, y Cortes de

Canteria, y que pueda rayar qualquier genero de Arco, o de buelta. Este ya es punto Executoriado en esta Real Audiencia.

En esta Corte Mexicana ay dos generos de Maestros: Uno que llaman principal es el de las Reales fabricas de Su Magestad y otro que se llama menos principal, es el de la Nobilissima Ciudad El primero tiene asu cargo las obras pertenecientes al Rey. Su sueldo anteriormente eran 600 pesos los quatrocientos por la obra matherial de la Santa Yglesia Cathedral, y los doscientos restantes para el Real Palacio; con este sueldo se mantubo esta Plaza hasta en tiempo del Señor Conde de Revilla Gigedo que mandó Su Magestad suspender la renta de la Santa Yglecia, dejandoles los dichos 200 pesos. Este es todo el Emolumento de esta Plaza, pues aunque su titulo expresa que gocen el sueldo con los demas emolumentos que les pertenecen por estas palabras no se hade entender que puedan percivir el precio de Maderas Viejas, y herrage etc. que se pueda expolear en dicho Real Palacio, sino solo la renta referida; Respecto alo qual es Plaza mui esquilmada en la conformidad que oy está.

Maior gravamen ha causado esta Plaza que Utilidad. Los Maestro Mayores que la han servido de 50 años a esta parte, pues ni aun aquel como interez que pudiera percivir de la compra de Matheriales, acaso por que los Dueños le querian bajar un medio, o una quartilla en Madera, Cal, etc. que ya se vee que esto es mui justo porque el Yngeniero, que siempre ha recidido en esta Ciudad ha tenido la mano lebantada para correr con los Matheriales, y firmarles las memorias para que su Excelencia dee el libramiento, y en su Vista les paguen en las Reales Caxas.

Pesar lo que puede cargar un Simiento

Suelese ofrecer que al Maestro lo llamen para una fabrica, y reconoce que pueden servir los Simientos Viejas por el grande ahorra de travajo, tiempo, Matherial etc. pidiese como averiguara se pueden toda via servir los Simientos.

Preparacion: como las Alas de toda la Mathematica, sean los experimentos prepare una vara cubica de aquel mismo mamposteado, y en el peso de la Romana aberique lo que pesa en el Ayre, y entonces hará el calculo de esta manera: operacion calcule el maziso de todas las Paredes, Calcule assi mismo el Maziso de techos con enladrillados, Bigas etc. Haga una suma en varas cubicas de todo, y multiplicando esto por los quintales que pesa una vara cubica, se tendra los quintales que cargan aquellos simientos.

Assi mismo porque el Maestro, tiene y echa la planta de la obra, vea assi mismo las varas cubicas de que se hade componer, y si estas superan alos primeras, dirá el Maestro no poderse quedar aquellos simientos, pero sino superan dirá poderse quedar aquellos simientos en el mismo estado enque estan quitando la fabrica vieja y haciendo enrrasado sobre aquellos mismos simientos.

Dada un Pisiete cuio alto son ⅔ largo ¼ ancho ⅙. Pide se quantos Pisietes entran en una Pilastra de una vara cubica. Verbi gracia. Este problema es el Aquiles de los Maestros: se resuelve de esta manera, y es regla General para semejantes problemas de mazisos:

Operacion hallase el solido de el Pisiete: hallase el solido de la Pilastra, que ya se vee que es mayor, partase al solido del Pisieste y se sabran quantos entran.

Exemplo: dispongase el Pisiete en la forma de queta de esta manera, y por que para Cubicar se multiplica la latitud por la altura, y luego para el largo será la multiplicacion y solido del Pisiete.

Quiere decir esto que se dividimos la vara cubica en 72 partes, la una de ellas servá un Pisiete. Bamos ala segunda parte. Partase ¹⁄₇₂. Avos aun entero en esta forma: y por que un entero vale 72. En este caso no ay mas que decir, sino que entran 72. Pisietes en la misma Pilastra.

Nota Que assi como se Cubico el Pisiete, se deve Cubicar la Pilastra quando le determina demenciones: Verbi gratia que tenga 12 varas de alto, 4 de ancho, y 2 de largo, se hara la misma operacion.

Finalmente que tanto el dividor como el dividendo, deven ser se una misma denominacion.

Terminos de la Montea

1. Toda piedra labrada consta de seis Superficies.
2. La *Y.M.* doble interior. *F.G.H.* doble exterior.

3. Superficie *F.M.* Paramento y Cara anterior. Su opuesta. *F.H.* Paramento, o Cara interior. Las otras dos Superficies: *F.Y.H.M.* se llaman luchas, o juntas, la Superficie sobre quien asienta, y ajusta otra se suele especialmente llamar lecho, y lo que asienta sobre ella sobre lecho, ala Piedra que esta en medio de un Arco, o Bobeda; se llama Clabe, y las primeras a uno, y otro Pie, imcumbas, o bohores.

4. Simbria, o Serechon, es la Tabla, o Tablas, cortadas con la misma cavida del Arco.

5. Guomon, o Esquadra, es un instrumento bien conocido, compuesto de dos reglas que forman un angulo recto.

6. Saltarella, es un instrumento conocido, que se compone de dos reglas mobiles sobre un punto a modo de Compaz, con el qual se toma qualquier angulo, y se pasa a las Piedras.

7. Regla Cerche, o baibel, Escoda, Sincel, o Tallantes.

8. Tirantes de un arco, o Bobeda, es quando todas sus junturas, o hilados se encaminan asia un punto se dice que las Piedras tienen sus tirantes asia dicho punto.

9. Un Arco se dice mober de quadrado quando la primera pie-dra de uno, y otro Pie del Arco asientan a Nibel y sobre el plano oriental.

10. Quando asientan sobre el plano inclinado, se dice mober de Salmer.

El Santuus Santa Santorum, fue segun los Hebros el lugar mas Secreto del Templo, dondo ninguno entraba sino era el Sumo Sacer-dotte.

Machinista: leg. si putater ad leg. aquilig. Es aquel que hace Machinas: pero segun Ulpiano leg. ult. d. simens falie. etc. Se dice el medidor: adiferencia del desempedrador que es el que mide los Campos con una pertica que tiene 10 pies.

De los examenes Hablaremos

Del Arte, sus profesores, y las ordenanzas que deven obserbar.

Nunca ha subido de ocho, ni bajado de quatro el numero de Maestros, en estta corte: Cosa que causa admiracion quando veemos en otros Exercicios, la copia de Yndividuos que los componen ha-game cargo de que con ocho ay numero suficiente para todas las obras que se puedan ofrecer. Es exercicio que necesita de una comun noticia, y assi veemos que algunos professores aunque ayan heredado el Arte, de sus Padres, viben descapados, por que no los conocen, y no es como en otros Exercicios que con hacerse patentes consiguen el credito de sus antessores.

Es arte como los demas liberales pero en esta Tierra se a echo gremio. Sacan Angel la Semana Santa, y estan obligados a marchar en forma quando lo pide la necessidad de alguna Guerra, y por este motibo tiene señalado Capitan, y demas oficiales conforme lo pide el Orden de Milicia; con titulo del Capitan General Excelentisimo Señor Virrey. No me acuerdo haver leido que gozen algun privilegio como se mira en otros Artes.

En el corte de Madrid, un manzebo Franzes que no llegaba a 23 años servia la Plaza de Maestro Mayor con sueldo de ocho mil pesos = tiene Uniforme con Baston, Casa en el Real Palacio, y el Coche de Camara de Su Magestad. Lo qual deviera hacer patente asu Excelencia el Maestro Maior de sus Reales Fabricas para que le subieran el Salario.

Nombres genericos para que el Maestro sepa dar una declaracion en su Lugar

1. Quien hade negar que de aqui pende que al Maestro le paguen bien, por que una declaracion bien dada en concurso de los otros Maestros: como estos ignoren lo que son puntos de derecho, no luzen tanto como la de el Architecto Jurista, por que persuade y da razon cabal del punto sobre que se puede hablar. Aqui resumo todo quanto se puede desear en la materia.

Edificio se dice = quasi edium factio, et est. edium constructio: aunque tambien ser surpa = pro omni structura: En su apelacion, segun Ulpiano Leg. si fund. qui fundis de legatis. 1. se entiende no tanto la superficie, sino tambien el suelo en donde esta construido o fabricado el Edificio: edificare est eq. facere, secu construere, se toma pro reficere: Esto es, rehacer, o redificar. Leg. 2a de Mortis inferendis. Edificio continente est id. atq. continum seu continuatis Leg. 1 d. de ag pluv. ancend. el leg urbis appell. de vento. Significat: I por que como el Edificio contenga bajo de si; edes dimune que es la casa casamentiz forum, havitatienz tabernes se le de al Architecto razon de la propia significacion de cada cosa en esta manera.

3. El Nombre lotes que allí no se a Aplicado consta de dospartes, segun Juristas, combiene a saver el suelo y la superficie Leg.

solumd. de revend. Se entiende por superficie todo lo que esta edificado sobre la Tierra.

Los Maestros para serlo Deven ser Examinados en forma portante el Escrivano de Cabildo, que es quien autoriza el titulo, o Carta de Examen: Los dos veedores electos de aquel año; deven serciorarse de su Suficiencia, trato de geometria, practica, como Especulativa, y de Aretmetica; no pide este Examen que sean ni ayan sido operarios, ni Albañiles, y este ya es punto executoriado por un Don Diego Davila, Contador de la Santa Yglecia que siguio el Litis contra los veedores de su tiempo pues haviendose querido examinar, se lo impidieron, y esta Real Audiencia visto el parecer Fiscal, Libro Executoria para que se examinen de la Suficiencia Geometria; pero esto no quita que en el Examen de la obra se les pueda pedir por los veedores, que asienten una Pilasta, ni un tramo de corniza por que como ya esten cortadas las Piedras con la montea que habra dado el mismo Maestro. Este travajo no mancha como no ha manchado alos Septros y Coronas que se han empleado en la Colocacion de los primeras piedras de los Templos: para este efecto se les hace Cuchara de plata, u oro, segun fuere el Personage.

Por lo que toca a gastos de Examen son 100 pesos con lo que tiene bastantes para el refresco, y gastos de Justicia, la media annata no sube a ocho pesos, son equiparables en orden a este punto con los demas oficios mecanicos, si son examinados quod, o como ellos dicen de lo blanco, tienen facultad para entender en todo genero de tazaciones para que fueren nombrados por los Tribunales Ecleciasticos, y seculares; pero si son Examinados de lo prieto, que assi llaman al que examinan sin saver ler, y escrivir, solo deven entender en Casas de Abode, sin que puedan meterse a el Calculo de Tazaciones, y no vale que otro lo haga por el.

Por lo tocante al Maestro Mayor que da ya expuesta su obligacion, pero aqui de paso me ha parecido noticiar que ay un Juez de obras (que segun e tenido noticio sirbe la Plaza de Vatse) Causa quiza de que se le agan algunos destajos pro el Maestro Mayor, y aunque no es obligacion del Maestro servirle pero en tanto que paga el material de sus obras, no hara mucho el Maestro en poner su travajo toda la Vez que tiene la seguridad de Escudarse para muchos acontecimientos de los respectos del señor Juez de Obras. Esta es por lo que toca al Maestro Maior de las Reales fabricas.

Por lo tocante al Maestro de la Ciudad, lo es tambien del Real Desague, cuya vista de ojos que se hace no le incumbe de obligacion, ni al Yngeniero ni al Maestro Mayor (salvo caso eminente de enundacion) sino solo al Maestro Mayor de Ciudad, que percibe sueldo por la obra de el Real Desague: Dixe que salvo caso de eminente peligro de inundacion, por que en este caso estan obligados todos los Peritos del Arte anivelar tantear, y reconocer el pendiente de Agua lo qual se practica con Oydores se asistencia, y Decreto de su Excelencia para poder desbaratar y demoler qualquier fabrica, fundo etc. aunque Sea de los Ecleciasticos.

En quanto al Govierno Politico de esta Plaza este advertido el Yngeniero, y el Maestro Mayor que sus Exas no dan libramiento de corto interes, supuesto que esperan aque sea cantidad notable la que sea gastado: por que como sean de poca monta algunos remiendos que se ofrezcan Verbi gratia blanqueo de una pieza. o sala etc. Fuera impertinencia del Maestro pedir libramiento para una cosa tan corta.

Edificios del Especial Nota

Un Hospital hade tener Pila, las Enfermerias inmediatas, a Enfermeros, y Capellanes: la entrada de los de la calle, a los viviendas de Capellanes, y Enfermeros, no hade ser por las mismas Enfermerias como la Despenza, Cozina, y Atoleria etc.

Un Palacio (dicen que asu maior eminencia ninguna fabrica puede subir) = Es parte de sus constitucion: Carceles, Calabozos, con Ventanas para que entre el Sol por ellas alos Pobres aprisionados, Pila, Veques, Lugares o Letrinas, ala vista de todos, Capilla, u Oratorio, de Elevazion eminente, las Paredes gruesos duplo, que lo comun, Simientos lo mismo etc. Panaderias, oficinas necessarios: Quartos amodo de quarteles para Peones.

Tozineria consta por Experiencia que los Piojos de Puerco taladran las Paredes.

Combentos merced de Agua
Templo con Cruzero: hade tener de largura quatro anchos del suio.

Sin Cruzero lo mismo por lo menos.

Si con Cruzero al Cuerpo de la Yglecia dos quadros y medio;

siguese el Simborrio que hade tener 1 con la Cupula, y luego se sigue el Presbiterio que se le dara un quadro: con que en este caso tendrá todo el Templo quatro quadro y medio.

Con cinco quadros quedan 3 hasta el Cruzero, uno al Simborrio y otro al Presbiterio, y esto es lo mejor. Quenta redonda.

Vamos ahora al Cruzero: este pues tendrá por cada lado la mitad del ancho de la Nave.

Lo mismo se dice de las Capillas, que tendran de profundo la mitad de el ancho de la Nave.

Si en Templo constare de tres Naves, los dos de los lados, cada una tenga de ancho la mitad de la de en medio.

En quarto agruesos de las medidas expresadas se deve incluir la espesura de Paredes; Vease la figura siguiente.

$O.B.$ es el ancho a descression del Arquitecto.

En la linea $O.A.$ se cuentan cinco anchos y que da el paralelo como $A.B.$ figura que tendra el Templo, los tres quadros has H es M el Cuerpo de la Yglecia, siguese el Cruzero que tendra un quandro $Y.E.$ y el Presbiterio $D.B.$ otro quadro el Cruzero $C.G.$ sale fuera del quadro todo lo que dice $C.D.$ que es la mitad de la $O.B.$ por cada lado.

El Architecto deve sacar tres plantas o descripciones, de qual-quiera edificio: que sean Sehnografica = Othografica = Seno-grafica. Descripcion ignografica, es la que delinea la planta de la Edificio. Orthografica, es la que descrive el Perfil y Sienografica, es la que pinta emprespectiva.

Ladrillos: ni sobrado crudos, ni tampoco mui cosidos, por que si estan mui cosidos, se hacen vidriosos, y si sobrados crudos, no resisten las inclemencias de el Tiempo, y se desbaratan con solo el piso en breve tiempo.

Tepes o Zespedes, son pedasos de Tierra mui travajada con raizes de la Grama; y al adove se le ministra Paja para su mayor trabazon, la especie de Adove no son para Paredes.

Alcobas se hacen quadrados: Piezas de servicio la deagonal de el quadrado, y de ancho el largo del mismo quadrado, las Ante Salas y piezas de recivimiento tendran proporcion sesquatierra, esto es su ancho dos tercias de su largo. Las Salas de Estado quardaran la razon de 7 a 4 y las que han de servir para saraos, o banquetes tendran su largo duplo, de su ancho y todas han de estar su quadro, algo mas de altura.

Calerias—son la Calera, o los Hornos para hazer Cal.

Cisterna—Es el conceptaculo donde se recogen las Aguas.

Teatro—Aherando impicundo, es voz Griega significa lugar para representar.

Amphiteatro—Es el Theatro, pero en todo rigor es el lugar formando de dos Theatros.

Canteras—el Jurista les dice latemias. Sucurrio: excausis. Lugar donde se cortan Piedras.

Alberca—Pizina, Lugar donde se nutren y conserban las Aguas.

Chafranado dira, y no achaflanado.

Derramos dira, y no derrames.

Excavar. Lo mismo que cabar, sacar tierra.

Calcujo. Aereomotico es el que se hace midiendo los solidos de Paredes etc.

Brocal: a el bordo de la Pila, u Pozo.

Glossary

The glossary includes principally the technical terms used in this manual, and it notes how the author's use of words differed from standard usage in the eighteenth century. It also notes changes in usage between that century and this. The 1726 edition of the Royal Academy's *Diccionario de autoridades,* the *Vocabulario arquitectónico ilustrado,* and Francisco Santamaria's *Diccionario de mejicanismos* were used in preparing the glossary.

abarrada. Dam.

abujón. Drafting protractor or mariner's compass used by architects to construct sundials.

accesorio. Shop located on the street level of a building.

acequia. Irrigation system.

achaflanado. A colloquialism or misspelling of *chaflanado,* which in the eighteenth century meant chamfered or beveled. See also *chafrando.*

acojinado. Cushion-shaped element used in the decorative detailing of a building. Synonymous with *almohadilla.*

adobe. Sun-dried bricks manufactured either as *de marca,* whose composition was regulated, or as *sancopinca,* which was an inferior grade.

alarife. Architect.

alberca. Reservoir or *caja de agua.*

alcantarilla. The archaic meaning intended by the author is aqueduct. It is now used to mean a small bridge, culvert, drain, underground sewer, or, in Mexico City, a public fountain.

alcayata. Hook used with padlocks or windows, as the author uses the term in this manuscript. It can also refer to a spike.

alfardas. Used by the author to mean supporting beams for a non-vaulted staircase. It also refers to the walls of a staircase.

andamio. Scaffold.

antepecho. Railing, guardrail, sill, parapet, or breastwork.

arco. Arch.

arena. Sand.

arroba. A unit of weight equal to twenty-five pounds.

atravesado. Long ashlar made of *chiluca* or *cantería* in standard dimensions.

audiencia. Spanish judicial institution that was also responsible for political administration in the Spanish colonies. In cities where a *real audiencia* was in residence, no public work or building could be undertaken without the approval of its officials.

azadón. A type of iron bar weighing between five and six pounds used by smiths. See also *hierro.*

baivel. Instrument used by stonecutters in the eighteenth century which formed a *mixtilíneo* angle equal to that of the foundation stones or *salmeres* of an arch. Synonymous with *regla cercha* in the eighteenth century. Today a *baivel* is a square bevel used by stonemasons. A *mixtilíneo* arch is one whose outline is made up of both straight and curved lines.

barreta. Iron bar edged with steel that weighed nineteen pounds or more. Used by smiths. See also *hierro.*

baza. Technically, the pedestal or base of a column or pilaster above the plinth. Here it appears to refer to the plinth itself.

bohar. Synonymous with *incumba,* according to the author. The word *bohar* may have been a colloquialism, since it is not in the eighteenth-century dictionary. The accepted term was *bolsón,* which was the first stone laid in the construction of an arch.

bolsón. The first stone laid in the construction of an arch; the same as *salmer* or *incumba.*

bolzor. Possibly a colloquialism for *bolsón,* the first stone laid in the construction of an arch.

braza. Eighteenth-century unit of measurement regulated as a six-foot length. The author, however, in referring to *brazas* or *brazadas* of stone, specifies a square measurement of four varas by two varas.

brazada. A term apparently used by the author as a synonym for *braza,* which was eight square varas of stone.

brocal. Curbstone of a fountain or well.

cabildo. Municipal government. Among its jurisidictions which touched upon the architect's profession were maintaining public buildings and roads and overseeing the guilds.

caja de agua. Reservoir.

cal. Lime.

calafatear. To caulk.

calería. Lime kiln.

canefa. A border, usually painted. Also spelled *zanefa* in the eighteenth century.

canero. Upper rail of a door. The term today applies to all kinds of rails of a door. See also *peinazones.*

cantería. Stone suitable for faceting which came in two qualities: *chiluca* (harder) and *cantería* (softer).

cantero. Stonecutter.

capataz. Overseer or maestro on a construction job.

cara anterior. Exposed vertical surface of a cut stone. See also *paramento.*

cara interior. Hidden vertical surface of a cut stone. See also *paramento.*

carga. Cartload.

carta de examen. License issued by the *cabildo* to a craftsman who has passed the examination to become a master of his craft.

cascajo. Old mortar reused as a sealer. Its present-day meaning is gravel or debris.

cateto. The two sides forming the right angle in a right triangle. The author, however, uses it to mean any line perpendicular to the foundation of a building.

cepa. Hole excavated for the foundation of a structure. See also *zepa.*

cerchon. Wooden support used to construct an arch. See also *cimbria.*

cerco. Possibly a colloquialism for the stile of a door. The term used now is *larguero.*

céspedes. Adobe bricks made from blocks of sod mixed with grass roots and straw. See also *tepes.*

chafrando. A colloquialism or misspelling of *chaflanado,* which in the eighteenth century meant chamfered or beveled. *Chaflanado* is the correct modern term.

chiluca. Hard stone suitable for faceting. See also *cantería.*

chumacera. Sill or lintel drilled with holes to seat a pintle door. The male element is called a *quisialera,* the female element a *tejuelo.*

cimbria. Eighteenth-century term for the wooden support used to construct an arch. Synonymous with *cerchon,* according to the author. The modern term is *cimbra.*

cimientos. Foundations.

cincel. Chisel.

claro. Width of a door or width between two elements (such as the width between arches).

clave. Keystone of an arch or vault.

clavos de media naranja. Half-orange nails; the equivalent of today's rose nail heads.

colorado. Red stone which was apparently suitable for faceting. See also *cantería* and *chiluca.*

columna. Column.

coluna. Column; accepted eighteenth-century spelling of *columna.*

cordeles. Hemp cords, used for surveying land or measuring buildings, that were marked in varas or fractions of varas.

corregidor. Vice governor with both political and judicial authority who administered a portion of a province (*gobierno*).

corridas. Stones presumably used in the frieze of an entablature.

cortina. Curtain wall.

danza de arcos. Succession of arches.

dedo. One forty-eighth of a Castillian vara, or approximately one-half inch.

de lo blanco. Master mason who was licensed to build in all media and to make appraisals.

de lo prieto. Master mason who was restricted to building with adobe and was prohibited by guild ordinance from making appraisals.

derrames. The splay of a door or window.

derramos. The splay of a door or window.

dovela exterior. Stonecutter's term indicating the convex facet of a voussoir. The term now used is *trasdos* (extrados in English).

dovela interior. Stonecutter's term indicating the concave facet of a voussoir. The term now used is *intradós* (intrados or soffit in English).

duelas. Floorboards.

empedrador. Maestro charged with the task of paving a room or street.

escalera de bóveda. Staircase built over a vault.

escalones. Stair treads. Also called *peldaños* or *huellas.*

escoda. Stonecutter's hammer.

escuadra. Carpenter's or mason's square.

esquinas. Stones used to describe an outside corner of a decorative element of a building.

estacamento. Staking a site or, in Mexico City, implanting wooden pilings under the footings necessary in the marshy substrate.

estuche de dibujo. Drafting set containing compass, angle rule, ruler, and other instruments.

guijarro. Hard, rounded stone or cobble found only in Tacubaya.

hierro. Iron for smithing, which came in several forms. The *barreta* was a bar edged with steel that weighed nineteen pounds or more. The *azadón* was a lighter bar weighing between five and six pounds. Another type was the *rodadillo,* but the author offers no description of it.

huacal. A burden basket that was also used as a dry measure in the building trade.

huellas. Risers of a staircase (*peraltes* or *contrahuellas* in today's usage), as used by the author. Today *huellas* (also called *escalones* or *peldanos*) refer to the steps themselves.

incumba. The first stone laid in the construction of an arch. Synonymous with *bohar* (*bolsón*), as used by the author. It is not in the eighteenth-century dictionary but was used by Tosca. The term used today is *bolsón* or *salmer.*

ingletes. Moldings describing a 45-degree angle.

juez del desagüe. Justice of the Royal Drainage Ditch of Huehuetoca charged with overseeing the maintenance of the ditch. He was evidently an *oidor* of the audiencia.

juez de obras. Justice of public works who was an *oidor* of the audiencia charged with overseeing public building construction in any city where an audiencia was located.

junta. Stonecutter's term for one facet that joins another. See also *lecho*.

ladrillo. Fired brick. *Ladrillo de marca* and *ladrillo común* both had standardized dimensions. Apparently there were two grades, refired and recolored, of the higher-fired *ladrillo de marca;* and two grades, red and orange, of the lower-fired *ladrillo común*.

laja. A unit of volume by which *tezontle,* volcanic stone used in building, was sold.

lechada. Whitewash.

lecho. Stonecutter's term for one facet that joins another. Synonymous with *junta*.

linea. Literally a boundary, but used by the author to mean the area of a surface.

lozas. Flagstones cut in fractions of varas. They were also called *tenayucas,* after the location where they were mined.

lucha. Possibly a colloquialism for *lecho* or *junta,* a stonecutter's term describing one facet that abuts another.

lumbrales. Lintels and doorsills or wood planks cut for that purpose.

maestro. A guild master, a position attained after a long training period as apprentice and journeyman. A maestro mayor was responsible for a monumental building venture such as a cathedral, or for a category of structures, such as the public works of Mexico City.

mampostería. Rubble construction, usually of small stones but sometimes containing broken brick as well, that was usually disguised by plaster and paint.

mediania. Common wall shared by two buildings.

merced. Royal grant of land or water rights.

mescla. Mortar. The author identified four grades: *la real* (royal), *mescla segunda* (second-quality), *mescla fina* (fine), and *mescla terciada* (mortar made of three ingredients).

michinales. Putlogs or *almojayas* left in a wall after scaffolding had been removed.

mocheta. Cornerstone or quoin.

moldado. Concave element used in building embellishments.

moldura. Moldings.

morillo. Wooden pole.

mover de quadrado. The spring from the impost of an arch.

mover de salmer. The spring of an arch from its *salmer,* the first stone laid in the construction of an arch.

oficial. Journeyman in a guild.

oidor. Judge of the audiencia.

padrino de la pared. Literally "the wall's godfather"; refers to the plane of a wall.

paramento. The surface treatment of a facade of a building. Also the vertical surfaces of a stone, which were also designated the *cara anterior* and *cara interior.* Today the two vertical facets of a stone are referred to as *babezas.*

pared. Load-bearing wall.

pasamanos. Handrail.

peinazones. Lower rails of a door. Also called *caneros,* according to the author. Both terms appear to have been only locally used in the late eighteenth century, for they are not found in the 1726 dictionary and are not used today.

peinazos. Upper rails of a door. The term today applies to all the rails of a door.

peon. Day laborer who was hired on a construction job but was not a guild member.

petril. Variation of *pretil* used in the eighteenth century to mean a balustrade or battlement.

piedra. Hard stone purchased by the *braza.*

pies derechos. Vertical supporting members of a building such as columns, jambs, or pilasters.

pisietes. Faceted stones of *chiluca* or *cantería* cut to smaller dimensions than *atravesado.*

pretil. Balustrade or battlement.

puesto. A public stall owned by the city and leased to a merchant or businessman.

quisialera. The male element of the sill or lintel of a pintle door. See also *chumacera.*

regidor. Councilman or alderman of the *cabildo.*

regla cercha. Instrument used by stonecutters in the eighteenth century that formed a *mixtilíneo* angle. A *cercha* is now a wooden rule for measuring convex or concave objects. See also *baivel.*

rejas. Door or window grills made of wood or iron.

rincones. Stones used to describe an inside cut corner angle of a decorative element of a building.

ripio. Crushed stone or brick used as grog in mortar.

rodadillo. Iron bar used by smiths. See also *hierro.*

rodapie. Skirting added to reinforce a footing.

salmer. Stone cut with one inclined edge and used as the first unit in an arch or vault springing from the impost. The author, however, uses it to mean a voussoir generally.

saltaregla. Hinged ruler with a semicircular device for reading angles.

saltarella. Alternate spelling of *saltaregla.*

sancopinca. An inferior grade of *adobe.*

sardinel. The threshold of a door. It is also used to describe brick set on edge to form a molding.

sobrebaza. Term used by the author to refer to the rounded element (*baza*) upon which a column or pilaster is seated.

sobre lecho. Stonecutter's term for one facet which lies atop another.

solera. Foundation plate upon which the floor joists rest.

suelo. Floor.

tabique. Partition, non–load-bearing wall.

tabla. Board.

tabla de techar. Ceiling board.

tajamanil. Wood shingles.

talud. Part of the footing for a wall exposed above the foundation level, but wider than the wall itself.

taluz. Used by the author to mean *talud.*

tapial. Wooden barricade around a construction site.

tenayuca. Flagstone (*loza*) named after the settlement (Tenayuca) where it was mined.

tepes. Adobe bricks made from blocks of sod mixed with grass roots and straw.

terraplenar. To fill any hollow space in a structure, such as the inside of a *mampostería* wall, with earth or other material.

tezonclale. Alternate spelling of *tezontlale.*

tesoncle. Alternate spelling of *tezontle.*

tezontlale. A mortar made from the volcanic rock *tezontle.*

tezontle. A volcanic rock used for building in Mexico both in pre-Columbian and colonial times. A harder variety and a softer variety were available. Like hard stone, it was bought by the *braza.*

tirantes. The orientation toward a vanishing point of the joints of the stones in an arch or vault. The term is now used to indicate a joist or tie-beam.

trasdos. Used by the author apparently as a corrupted form of extrados, the

vara. A unit of lineal measurement that approximated three feet but varied slightly from region to region. Calibrated into halves, thirds, fourths, sixths, eighths, and dedos.

veedor. An elected overseer of a guild who assisted in examining the journeyman seeking his master's license.

viage. Weight carried from one place to another in a single trip, which varied according to the number of containers used and the product itself.

vigas. Beams.

xalpaco. A watery mortar used as an undercoat for whitewash.

zaguan. Entryway located in the center of a facade with sufficient width and height to admit horses and carriages into the patio.

zanjas. Trenches.

zepa. Hole excavated for the foundation of a structure. See also *cepa.*

zulaque. Pitch used to seal pipe joints.

Bibliography

Alberti, Leone Battista. *Ten Books on Architecture.* 1755. Reprint, edited by Joseph Rykwert. London: Alec Tirante, Ltd., 1955.

Apenas, Ola. *Mapas antiguas del valle de México.* Mexico City: Universidad Nacional Autónoma de México, Instituto de Historia, 1947.

Barrio Lorenzot, Francisco del. *Ordenanzas de gremios de la Nueva España.* Mexico City: Talleres Gráficos, 1920.

Benjamin, Asher. *The American Builders Companion or, a System of Architecture Particularly Adapted to the Present Style of Building.* 1827. Reprint. New York: Dover Publications, Inc., 1969.

Berlin, Heinrich. "Artifices de la catedral de México." *Anales del Instituto de Investigaciones Estéticas* 11 (1944): 19–39.

Bibliographie général de l'astronomie. 2 vols. 1889. Reprint. London: The Holland Press, 1964.

The Builder's Dictionary: or Gentleman and Architect's Companion. 2 vols. 1734. Reprint. Washington: Association for Preservation Technology, 1981.

Carrera Stampa, Manuel. *Los gremios mexicanos.* Mexico City: Ibero-Americana de Publicaciones, 1954.

———. *Planos de la Ciudad de México.* Boletín de la Sociedad Mexicana de Geografía y Estadística, vol. 67, nos. 2–3. Mexico City: 1949.

Cartografía de ultramar. Carpeta III: Mexico. 2 vols. Madrid: Imprenta del Servicio Geográfico del Ejército, 1955.

Diccionario enciclopédico Espasa. Madrid: Espasa-Calpé, S.A., 1978.

Diccionario enciclopédico hispano-americana. London: C. H. Simonds, n.d.

Diccionario enciclopédico UTEHA. Mexico City: Unión Tipográfica, Editorial Hispano-Americana, 1950–64.

Diccionario Porrua: Historia, biografía y geografía de México. 2 vols. Mexico City: Editorial Porrua, S.A., 1976.

Durant, Will. *Caesar and Christ*. Vol. 3 of *The Story of Civilization*. New York: Simon and Schuster, 1944.

Enciclopedia del arte en América. Argentina: Bibliográfica Omeba, 1968.

Enciclopedia universal ilustrada: Europeo-América. Madrid: José Espasa-Calpé, n.d.

González Angulo, Jorge, and Yolanda Terán Trillo. *Planos de la Ciudad de Mexico, 1785, 1853 y 1896*. Mexico City: Instituto Nacional de Antropología e Historia, Departamento de Investigaciones Históricas, 1976.

Haring, C. H. *The Spanish Empire in America*. New York: Harcourt Brace Jovanovich, 1975.

Knoop, Douglas, and G. P. Jones. *The Medieval Mason: An Economic History of English Stone Building in the Later Middle Ages and Early Modern Times*. 1933. Reprint. New York: Barnes & Noble, Inc., 1967.

Kubler, George. *Arquitectura de los siglos XVII y XVIII*. Vol. 14 of *Ars Hispaniae*. Madrid: Editorial Plus-Ultra, 1957.

Llaguno y Amerola, Eugenio. *Noticias de los arquitectos y arquitectura desde su restauración*. 4 vols. Madrid: En la Imprenta Real, 1829.

Maza, Francisco de la. "El proyecto para la capilla de la Inquisición." *Anales del Instituto de Investigaciones Estéticas* 12 (1945): 19–26.

Meyer, Michael C., and William L. Sherman. *The Course of Mexican History*. New York: Oxford University Press, 1979.

Olvera C., María del Carmen. "La biblioteca de un arquitecto de la epoca virreinal en Mexico." *Monumentos Históricos*, no. 6 (1981): 33–40.

Palladio, Andrea. *The Four Books of Architecture*. 1738. Reprint. New York: Dover Publications, Inc., 1965.

Real Academia Española. *Diccionario de autoridades*. 1726. Reprint. Madrid: Editorial Gredos, 1969.

———. *Diccionario de la lengua española*. Madrid: Real Academia Española, 1984.

Recopilación de leyes de los reynos de las Indias. 4 vols. 1681. Reprint. Madrid: Ediciones Hispánica, 1973.

Renard, George. *Guilds in the Middle Ages*. London: G. Bell and Sons, Ltd., 1919.

Rivera Cambas, Manuel, ed. *Los gobernantes de México*. 2 vols. 1873. Reprint. Mexico City: Joaquín Porrua, S.A., 1981.

San Miguel, Andrés. *Obras de Fray Andrés de San Miguel*. Edited by Eduardo Baez Macias. Mexico City: Universidad Nacional Autónoma de México, Instituto de Investigaciones Estéticas, 1969.

Santamaria, Francisco J. *Diccionario de mejicanismos.* Mexico City: Editorial Porrua, S.A., 1974.

Serlio, Sebastiano. *The Five Books of Architecture.* 1611. Reprint. New York: Dover Publications, Inc., 1982.

Torre Revello, José. "Tratados de arquitectura utilizados en Hispanoamerica (siglos XVI a XVIII)." *Revista Interamericana de Bibliografía* 6, no. 1 (1956): 5–23.

Tosca, Tomás Vicente. *Tratados de arquitectura civil, montea y canteria y reloxes.* Valencia: La Oficina de los Hermanos de Orga, 1694.

Toussaint, Manuel. *Colonial Art in Mexico.* Translated and edited by Elizabeth Wilder Weismann. Austin: University of Texas Press, 1967.

———. *La Catedral de México.* Mexico City: Editorial Porrua, S.A., 1973.

"Una carta del arquitecto Ignacio de Castera." *Anales del Instituto de Investigaciones Estéticas* 10 (1943): 82–83.

Vitruvius Pollio, Marcus. *Vitruvius: The Ten Books on Architecture.* 1914. Reprint, translated by Morris Hicky Morgan. New York: Dover Publications, Inc., 1960.

Vocabulario arquitectónico ilustrado. Mexico City: Secretaria del Patrimonio Nacional, 1976.

Woolfe, John, and James Gandon. *The British Architect: Containing Plans, Elevations, and Sections; of the Regular Buildings Both Public and Private in Great Britain.* Vols. 4 and 5 of *Vitruvius Britannicus.* 1767. Reprint. New York: Benjamin Blou, Inc., 1967.

Index

About the Translator

MARDITH K. SCHUETZ has had years of experience as an archaeologist of Spanish colonial sites and as a historian of Northern Spain's northern borderlands. Since receiving her Ph.D. from the University of Texas, Austin, in 1980, she has devoted most of her time to the study of Spanish colonial architecture.